Spiritual Warfare

Understanding that there is a war being wage for soul of humanity!

By
Pastor James L. Monteria

CLM Publications & Publishing, LLC
P.O. Box 932
Chesterfield, VA 23832

www.clmpublication.info

All rights reserved.

No part of this book may be reproduced without written permission from the publisher except for use of brief review for furthering of the Kingdom of God unless otherwise indicated; all Scriptures are taken from the King James Version of the Bible

ISBN: 978-0-9897704-0-8

Cover Design/Graphics: Shelly E. Middleton

Author: James L. Monteria

Associate Editor: Mrs. Carrie Gay

Published by CLM Publications & Publishing, LLC

Copyright © 2014 by CLM Publications & Publishing, LLC Printed in the United States of America; All rights reserved under International Copyright Law. Contents and cover may not be reproduced in whole or in part in any form without the expressed written consent of the publisher.

Table of Contents

Acknowledgement	Page IX
Foreword	Page X
Guidelines for this Study	Page XI
Special note to you as the reader!	Page XIV
Introduction	Page 1
Chapter 1 What is Spiritual Warfare?	Page 4
A. Creation of Man and the fall of Man, and satan assumption of Power	Page 6
(1) What was given to mankind based upon Genesis 1:26-67.	Page 7
(2) In the fall of man, what power did the devil gains.	Page 8
B. What was the Mission of Jesus Christ?	Page 8
(1) In the midst of warfare what was Mission	Page 8
(2) To Restore order - ruler of God's Kingdom on earth	Page 11
(3) Jesus "Inherit" as a result of His victory on the Cross	Page 12
Chapter 2 Basic Training Part 1	Page 14
A. Kingdom in conflict	Page 15
1. The Kingdom of God (Heavenly Father, God the Son, and God the Holy Spirit.	Page 15
B. The Commander-in-Chief	Page 16
C. Angels	Page 17
(1) Execute God's judgment on the earth	Page 17
(2) Help God's people	Page 18
(3) Give instructions	Page 18

(4) Respond to prayer	Page 18
(5) Strengthen people	Page 19
(6) People	Page 19

Chapter 3 Basic Training Part 2 — Page 20

A. What is our Identity in Christ — Page 20
B. What are we commission to do? — Page 21

Chapter 4 The Armor of God (Dress for Success) — Page 25

A. The Belt of Truth — Page 25
B. The Breast Plate of Righteousness — Page 26
C. The Shoes of the Gospel of Peace — Page 27
D. The Shield of Faith — Page 28
E. The Helmet of Salvation — Page 30
F. The Sword of the Spirit — Page 31
G. Praying through the Armor of God with all prayers — Page 33

Chapter 5 Warfare Disciplines — Page 36

(1) God as the Master Trainer — Page 36
(2) People as Trainers — Page 37
(3) Disciplines to promote combat readiness — Page 38

A. Quiet Time — Page 40
B. Testing Doctrine, spirits, and people — Page 42
C. Controlling our thoughts — Page 42
D. Exercising Godliness — Page 36
E. A. Prayer is the Christians lifeline — Page 44

Chapter 6 Exposing the kingdom of Darkness — Page 48

A. The Kingdom of Darkness (devil) — Page 48
B. The commander and chief — Page 48
C. Evil Angels — Page 50
D. What are the snares of the devil? — Page 53

Chapter 7 List of strongmen and associated Spirits   Page 63
A.   Spirit of Divination   Page 63
B.   Familiar Spirits   Page 63
C.   Spirit of Jealousy   Page 63
D.   Lying Spirit   Page 64
E.   Perverse Spirit   Page 64
F.   Spirit of Haughtiness   Page 65
G.   Spirit of Heaviness   Page 65
H.   Spirit of Whoredoms   Page 65
I.   Spirit of Infirmity   Page 66
J.   Deaf and Dumb Spirit   Page 66
K.   Spirit of Bondage   Page 67
L.   Spirit of Fear   Page 67
M.   Seducing Spirits   Page 67
N.   Spirit of Anti-Christ   Page 68
O.   Spirit of Error   Page 68

Chapter 8 Biblical Curses   Page 69

Chapter 9 Prayer a key in spiritual warfare   Page 72
A.   Prayer of Thanksgiving, Praise, and Worship.   Page 75
B.   Prayer of Petition\Faith   Page 84
C.   Prayer of Binding and Loosing   Page 85
D.   Prayer of Intercession   Page 88

Chapter 10 Authority and the Weapons of our warfare   Page 94
A.   The Word of God   Page 95
B.   The Blood of Jesus   Page 95
C.   The Name of Jesus   Page 97
     (1) Believer's rights in the name of Jesus   Page 97
     (2) Power of the Spirit of Prayer   Page 99
D.   Daily Confession of Protection   Page 101
     (1) Psalm 91 personalize   Page 101

E. The Armor of God	Page	102
(1) The Power of Praise and Worship	Page	103
F. The Holy Spirit and His Gifts	Page	104
G. The Peace of God is a weapon	Page	105

Chapter 11 The Law of Authority — Page 107
A. What is spiritual jurisdiction — Page 109
B. Three Authorities in one world — Page 110

Chapter 12 Levels of Authority in the Realm of the spirit — Page 114

A. God's Jurisdiction — Page 114
B. God's Jurisdiction and His will — Page 115
C. God's Jurisdiction and His Word — Page 118
D. God's Jurisdiction and Man's will — Page 120
   (1) God Has Chosen to Move through Man — Page 121
E. God's Jurisdiction and Faith — Page 123

Chapter 13 The Believer's Jurisdiction — Page 126
A. Our legal position of Authority — Page 126
   (1) The Boundary of the Spirit Realm — Page 128
   (2) The boundary of Faith — Page 129

Chapter 14 The devil Jurisdiction — Page 132
A. Defining the devil kingdom and his jurisdiction — Page 132
B. Jurisdiction over three groups of beings — Page 137
C. Believer's legally delivered from the devil jurisdiction. — Page 137
   (1) Seated in Heavenly Places (Positional) — Page 139

Chapter 15 Example for starting your day of warfare prayer. — Page 141
A. Worship (Heavenly FATHER) — Page 141
   (1) Enter into his gates with thanksgiving — Page 141
   (2) LORD JESUS CHRIST; — Page 144
   (3) BLESSED HOLY SPIRIT: — Page 146
B. Forgiveness — Page 149

C.	Pray for those in Authority (Federal Government and State).	Page	152
	(1) GOVERNMENT - FEDERAL	Page	153
	(2) Pray for Local Government (State)	Page	155
D.	Pray for the of Israel and the peace of Jerusalem	Page	158
E.	Pray for the Body of Christ and its Leadership	Page	159
F.	Pray for others as the Holy Spirit leads	Page	160
G.	Pray for your family	Page	160
	(1) Submitting yourself to Almighty God	Page	161
	(2) Breaking generational curse	Page	161
	(3) Applying the blood of Jesus to cover your family	Page	163
	(4) Releasing the blessing of God over yourself and family.	Page	164
H.	Daily Confession	Page	166
	(1) Confession of Favor	Page	166
	(2) Confession of Who I am in Christ	Page	169
	Monday - I walk in love and faith	Page	169
	Tuesday - I flow in the guidance of the Holy Spirit	Page	170
	Wednesday - I walk in miracle working power of God	Page	171
	Thursday- I am healed	Page	171
	Friday – All my needs are meet	Page	172
	Saturday - I walk in the Favor \ Wisdom of God	Page	173
	Sunday – I walking in the Blessing	Page	174
J.	Daily confession of Protection Psalm 91	Page	176
	Decision Page to receive Salvation, Fullness of the Holy Spirit	Page	178
	Endnotes	Page	181
	About the Author	Page	182

Acknowledgement

First and foremost, I would not even know God, or be able to write anything about Him, were it not for His grace and mercy! I have come to appreciate the grace of God, the Lordship of Jesus Christ, and the Holy Spirit's presence in my life and my ministry, even more than words could express.

Forward

There is an adversary to the Christians and their life style, and whether it is realized or not we are in a WAR, a war is being wage, and it is called Spiritual Warfare. Spiritual warfare is the conflict between good and evil. It is the ongoing battle between two diametrically opposed kingdoms: God's kingdom (good) and satan kingdom (evil). Though it is inherently a spiritual conflict, spiritual warfare also manifests in the natural realm of flesh and blood. Humans are caught in the center of this struggle and may participate on either position. The origin of the conflict between good and evil goes back before the creation of Man. One of God's most powerful angels, Lucifer who eventual became (satan/the devil) is playing a key role.

We as Christians are here to fulfill the destiny that was given to mankind and that is defined in GENESIS 1:26-28;

"Then <u>God said</u>, "Let Us make man in Our image, according to Our likeness; **let them have dominion** over the fish of the sea, over the birds of the air, and over the cattle, over all the earth and over every creeping thing that creeps on the earth." So God created man in His *own* image; in the image of God He created him; male and female He created them. Then God blessed them, and God said to them, "Be fruitful and multiply; fill the earth and subdue it; **have dominion over** the fish of the sea, over the birds of the air, and over every living thing that moves on the earth." Gen 1:26-28 (NKJV)

GUIDELINES FOR STUDY

A. Guidelines for Individual Study
1. Set aside a regular time each week when you can get alone with God and study the lessons in this manual.
2. Pray and ask the Lord to illuminate His Word to you as you study.
3. Look up each scripture and take time to think about (meditate on) the Word of God.
4. Move through the book at a steady pace and allow the Holy Spirit to minister to you personally.

B. Guidelines for Group Study
1. In Bible study group, it is important to have one leader, preferably a mature Christian, who can facilitate the study each week.
2. Determine a regular time and a quiet location for weekly group meetings to study the lessons in this manual.
3. Pray and ask the Lord to illuminate His Word each week.
4. Look up the scriptures and take turns reading them aloud.
5. Encourage each person to participate. Do not allow one person to dominate the discussion. Allow for group discussion and interaction during the lessons, but avoid distractions with unnecessary side issues.

6. Do not be in a hurry to complete the study; rather, maintain a steady pace through the lesson while allowing the Holy Spirit the freedom to minister to each individual in the group.

7. Assign the next lesson as homework each week. After the group members have completed their individual study, they will be more familiar with the material. Encourage group members to write down any questions they have and present them for discussion the next time you meet together.

Spiritually Dressed for Success
Ephesians 6:10-18;

"Finally, my brethren, be strong in the Lord, and in the power of his might. [11]Put on the whole armor of God that ye may be able to stand against the wiles of the devil. [12] For we wrestle not against flesh and blood, but against principalities, against powers, against the rulers of the darkness of this world, against spiritual wickedness in high *places*. [13]Wherefore take unto you the whole armor of God that ye may be able to withstand in the evil day, and having done all, to stand. [14]Stand therefore, having your loins girt about with truth, and having on the breastplate of righteousness; [15]and your feet shod with the preparation of the gospel of peace; [16]Above all, taking the shield of faith, wherewith ye shall be able to quench all the fiery darts of the wicked. [17]And take the helmet of salvation, and the sword of the Spirit, which is the word of God: [18]Praying always with all prayer and supplication in the Spirit, and watching thereunto with all perseverance and supplication for all saints;"

Special note to you as the reader!

Spiritual warfare *is the conflict between the devil and humankind. There is no contest between God and the devil. God could with one breathe, eliminate the devil forever; the devil has been defeated by Jesus the man of God. Spiritual warfare is the conflict between the devil and humankind. The devil hates the creation, God, humankind, because humankind has been made in the image of God.*

When you desire to gain knowledge about your enemy, there is always the possibility of confrontation or an attack. The reason for this is that the enemy does not want you to know his tactics and means of operation. However, the Bible says we should not be ignorant of his devices.

As a precautionary measure, I am going to list a couple of weapons that you will need when the attack occurs. You must have faith in these three weapons.

1. Faith in The **WORD OF GOD**, especially *Psalm 91*. A whole year prior to studying and teaching on spiritual warfare, the Holy Spirit instructed me read and confesses Psalm 91 over myself entire family on a daily base. *Hebrews 4:12*

2. Faith in The **BLOOD OF JESUS**. As a precautionary measure, I cover my entire family with the blood of Jesus on a daily bases morning, noon, and night.

3. Faith in The **NAME OF JESUS**. The most powerful name in the universe is Jesus, all

Luke 10:19

Authority has been given unto Him, and He has delegate that authority unto us that are born-again. *Acts 4:12, Acts 3:16, and Hebrews 9:12*

Spiritual Warfare
Introduction

In this *Work Book,* we are teaching on warfare. There many Christians that do not believe that we are in a war. From my spiritual perspective, there are four reasons why people go to church:

The traditional church goers Go to church to see who is there, to be noisy, or to have something to talk about; Another group of church goers, Go get a hookup, through networking, whether it is a business deal or a booty deal.

Another group of church goers, Go to hide because they are scared of what is going on out in the world and they think that these four walls will protect them; and Another group of church goers, Go to really seek after God to trying to obtain a better life and how to live in victory in this earth.

It is my prayer that all people attend church for the reason they can be refilled, and can get some spiritual fuel in their tanks so that they can go out and finish the work God has called them to do. In this book of teaching, we will go into the enemies' camp with the book of Ephesians. Ephesians is a book of warfare in which Paul is talking about doing battle in the spirit realm from earth. As we are here on this earth, there are things that we do not see.

There is more in the unseen realm than there is in the scene realm. I remember my dad saying, "If we only knew what was outside at night we would not even stick our head out at night". I know that there are things that we can look at in the natural realm, but there are much more in the unseen (invisible) realm. Whether we know or like this invisible realm is pretty much controlled by the demonic spirit.

As Christians and children of God, we are here to make a difference.

We are to take back what the devil and his co-laborers have stolen, and we are here to demonstrate his defeat in our lives, in our circumstances, and the environments that we are according to 1 John 3:8c "For this purpose the Son of God was manifested, that he might destroy the works of the devil." We have the same job that is to demonstrate that the devil is defeat.

In **Ephesians 2:1-2;** (KJV) "¹And you hath he quickened, who were dead in trespasses and sins; ²Wherein in time past ye walked according to the course of this world, according to the prince of the power of the air, the spirit that now worketh in the children of disobedience:

In **Ephesians 2:1-2**, (AMPV) ¹AND YOU [He made alive], when you were dead (slain) by [your] trespasses and sins ²In which at one time you walked [habitually]. You were following the course and fashion of this world [were under the sway of the tendency of this present age], following the prince of the power of the air. You were obedient to and under the control of the demon spirits that still constantly works in the sons of disobedience the careless, the rebellious, and the unbelieving, who go against the purposes of God.

The Holy Spirit is saying through the Apostle Paul that there are spirits that exist in this world; even as I speak there are some who are here to control this earth. These are the ones, who cause people to do things according to his agenda.

For example, rebellion is the result of influence cause by the devil and demons, and they are causing the one who are rebellious, because it is in line with his agenda, rather than having everyone follow the godly agenda of God.

In **Ephesians 2:3;** (AMPV) - Among these we as well as you once lived and conducted ourselves in the passions of our flesh our behavior governed by our corrupt and sensual nature], obeying the impulses of the flesh and the thoughts of the mind [our cravings dictated by our senses and our dark imaginings. We were then by nature children of God's wrath and heirs of His indignation, like the rest of mankind.

Therefore, it says here that the people that are under the sway of these demonic spirits are obeying, and being governed by their sensual nature. Everything to them is sensual nature, they are not walking according to the word of God, but they are walking according to the sensual nature, feelings, look good, the passion of the flesh, etc.

Chapter 1
What is Spiritual Warfare?

Spiritual warfare is the conflict between the devil and humankind. There is no contest between God and the devil. God could with one breathe, eliminate the devil forever; the devil has been defeated by Jesus, the man of God. Spiritual warfare is the conflict between the devil and humankind. The devil hates the creation, God, humanity because humankind has been made in the image of God.

It is an ongoing battle between two diametrically opposed kingdoms: God's kingdom (good) and satan kingdom (evil).

The origin of the conflict between good and evil goes back before the creation of Man. One of God's powerful angels, lucifer, played a key role.

Who is this person lucifer, satan, the devil, and the dragon. We have primarily three scriptures Ezekiel 28:12-13, Isaiah 14:12-15, and Revelation 12:7-9.

According to Ezekiel 28:12-13; and Isaiah 14:12-15; what are some details about lucifer original character, appearance and position?

- Model of perfection, Full of wisdom, Perfect in beauty
- Every precious stone was his covering
- He may have had a special role in worshipping God – head "tumbrels and pipes" built into his body
- He was in Eden
- God had ordained and anointed Lucifer as a guardian cherub He was on the holy mount of God, and walked among the fiery stones (around God's throne).

He was blameless being his ways since he was created, until sin was found in him
- Another reference to special function of worship – he had "harps"
- He was called morning star and son of the dawn

As we continue to examine the scriptures we find that lucifer was perfect until he made his first mistake and found the answer located in Ezekiel 28:15; "You were blameless in your ways from the day you were created till wickedness was found in you", and continue in Ezekiel 28:17-18; we find how his sin did affect him? Proud heart because of his beauty His splendor corrupted his wisdom.

His splendor corrupted his wisdom

- Many sins" and "dishonest trade" caused him to be filled with violence.

In reading Isaiah 14:12-15; we find five things lucifer purposed to do? In reading Revelation 12:3-9, we find another evil task that lucifer said.

1. Ascend to heaven
2. To raise his throne above the stars of God
3. Sit enthroned on the mount of assembly
4. Ascend above the tops of the clouds
5. To make himself like God - Deceived one third of God's angels (stars) to follow him

Now that we know from the scripture what lucifer said, let us see what God said to lucifer and his evil angels because of their sin of rebellion. In Ezekiel 28:16-19;

- Removed his beauty, disgraced him and made a spectacle of him before kings
- Expelled him from the mount of God
- Made fire come from within him and consume him; reduced him to ashes Isaiah 14:12-15; Revelation 12:7-9;
- Cast them out of heaven to earth and removed his power
- Brought him down to the pit

Summary

lucifer was in the Garden of Eden in the form of the serpent. Apparently, he had already rebelled against God, becoming satan (i.e. The Adversary). His goal was to deceive Eve and ultimately Adam.

A. Creation of Man and the fall of Man and satan assumption of power

Man was created to exercise power and designed to manage it. The motivating purpose for the creation of the human species was to dominate the earth and its resources. The result of the Creator desires to extend His rulership from the supernatural realm to the physical realm. His plan and program were to have a family of spiritual children. He would call His sons. The record of this creative act is found in Genesis 1:26-27.

Part 1. What was given to humanity based on Genesis 1:26-27?

Just a reminder of what happened in Genesis 1:26-27; in whose image and likeness did God create humans? Answer: In God's image.

In reading Genesis 1:26, 28; Psalm 8:4-8; we must understand what was given to humanity by God so that we can walk in as that has been restored back by the second Adam. It was an authority/power that God gave to man.

- Rule over the fish, birds, livestock, all the creatures of the earth, and over all of the earth
- The power to fill and subdue the earth
- Rule over the works of God's hands – everything was to be kept under man's authority.

Part 2. In the fall of man, what power did the devil gain?

In reading Genesis 3:17-19; 2 Peter 2:19; Romans 5:6; 12-14; 17; 20-21; we find three things that happened because of Adam and Eve sin?

- Adam (Mankind) came under a curse affecting the ground himself was to work, he was expelled from the garden and had to work on soil that was cursed with thorns and thistles.
- Adam (Mankind) became a slave to sin because he allowed sin to master him.
- Adam (Mankind) was stripped of his power.

Also, in reading Romans 8:19-20; How was the rest of creation affected by Adam and Eve's sin? It was subjected to frustration and bondage to decay.

In this same event what power and authority did the devil gain after deceiving man? Based upon Luke 4:5-6; Authority and power of all the world's kingdoms, and in John 12:31;

He is the current ruler of the world, in Ephesians 2:2; He is the "prince of the power of the air." According to Hebrews 2:14-15, and He gained the power of death and used the fear of death to enslave people and in 1 John 5:19; He is able to sway (deceive) the entire world with such an array of powers, it is easy to see how many people might fall under satan influence.

Thankfully, Jesus Christ came to undo the works of the devil. He brings salvation to all those who would believe on his name. Let us examine Christ's work, and how it affects those who believe in him.

B. What was the Mission of Jesus Christ?

Jesus came as a man to show how a man full of the Word of God and full of Spiritual warfare is the conflict between good and evil. It is the ongoing battle between two diametrically opposed kingdoms: God's kingdom (good) and satan kingdom (evil).

Though it is inherently a spiritual conflict, spiritual warfare also manifests in the natural realm of flesh and blood. Humans are caught in the midst of this conflict and may participate in the struggle on either side.

Part 1. In the mist of this warfare what was Jesus mission?

Jesus came as a man to show how a man full of the Word of God and full of the Holy Spirit, Jesus like a second Adam.

If we truly understand the mission of Jesus Christ, we would move from a defeatist mentality to a victorious mentality. The reason that so many Christians are undeveloped and defeated is that they do not truly understand that Christianity is a lifestyle and not a religion. Putting it briefly religion is nothing more than man attempts to get to God through keeping a set of rules and perform some rituals.

Jesus came to show us how humanity full of the Word of God, meaning they have the Word of God in their hearts, and not just in their heads.

See the way that you get the Word of God in your heart is by reading it on a daily base and recognizes that is food to your spirit, and that without it your spirit is weak, unnourished and you are a defeat going somewhere to happen.

Why?
1. Is by believing that the Bible is the Word of God.
2. By reading the Bible on a daily. Some have the nerve not, to the Word of God.
3. By studying the Word of God, putting yourself in a position so that the Holy Spirit can give you some revelation of the things of God.

Now that some of you may be a little, hot under the collar or convicted by the Holy Spirit. Let us see what Jesus mission was?

Jesus came as a man to show how a man full of the Word of God, and full of the Holy Spirit. In reading several of scriptures, I want to ask, how was Jesus like a second Adam?

> ***1 Corinthians 15:21-22;*** *Death came through Adam to all people; the resurrection of the dead (i.e. Life) comes through Jesus.*
> ***1 Corinthians 15:27;*** *He had dominion over all things; just as Adam originally had dominion over the earth and its creatures (Genesis 1:28).*
>
> ***1 Corinthians 15:45-47;*** *the first Adam became a living being; Jesus, the "last Adam," became a "life giving spirit".*
>
> ***Romans 5:12-19;*** *Sin and death entered the world through Adam; God's grace and gift of justification came through Jesus; Just as many were made sinners through the disobedience of one man, Adam, many will be made righteous through the obedience of one man, Jesus.*
>
> *1* ***Corinthians 15:22-28***, *as the "second Adam", what are Christ's objectives from now until the end times*

Part 2 To Restore order - ruler of God's kingdom on earth"

He is to restore order and ruler of God's kingdom both on earth and in the heaven; he will subdue all God's enemies and then turn over the kingdom to the Father.

In reading Luke 4:18-21, what was five of Jesus' initial mission objectives as he began his earthly ministry?

1. Preach the good news to the poor
2. Proclaim freedom for the prisoners
3. Proclaim recovery of sight for the blind
4. Release the oppressed
5. Proclaim the year of the Lord's favor

One of the first things people noticed about Jesus at the beginning of his ministry was that he preached the word of God with authority (Luke 4:31-32). Next, he demonstrated that authority in many different ways.

As we continue to examine the mission of Jesus; In reading Luke 4:33-37; 38-39; 4:40; Luke 5:4-8; 20-26; Luke 7:12-15; Luke 8:22-25; For these verses what did what Jesus do?
- Cast evil spirits out of people; Luke 4:33-37;
- Rebuked a high fever and it left; Luke 4: 38-39;
- Laid hands on people and healed them of various kinds of sickness; Luke 4:40;
- Demonstrated authority over all creation; a large catch of fish; Luke 5:4-8Forgave sins and healed a paralytic; Luke 5:20-26; Raised a widow's dead son; Luke 7:12-15; demonstrated authority over the wind and waves (the elements) Luke 8:22-25.

Part 3 "Jesus "inheritance" as a result of his victory on the cross and his resurrection"

What did Jesus "inherit" because of his victory on the cross and his resurrection?
According to Philippians 2:9-10.

Ephesians 1:20-23; and Hebrews 1:3-4.

- He was exalted to the highest place and received the name that is above every name.
- God seated him at his right hand in the heavenly realms and placed all things under his feet, and He became far superior to the angels.

In examining John 1:12; John 3:16; Romans 5:1; Romans 5:1; Romans 6:4-5; Romans 8:9-13; 16-17; What did Jesus accomplish on the cross for those who believe in him?

- Gave them the right for them to be called children of God
- Gave them eternal life
- Brought peace between them and God
- Enabled them to live a new life
- Enabled them to receive the Holy Spirit

Designated them heirs of God and co-heirs with Christ.

It is awesome to think that we are co-heirs with Jesus, with all the authority and power that he has. Unfortunately, some Christians do not fully understand the scope of their inheritance in Christ, or worse, they understand it but do not believe it. As with many aspects of the Christian walk, faith is the key to moving into our inheritance.

As we understand the mission of Jesus, we need to know that there are some things that have been conferred upon us. In reading Matthew 28:18-20; and Genesis 1:28; what mission did Jesus confer upon us as his believers to carry out on earth? In addition, how is our mission similar to Adam and Eve's mission prior to The Fall?

- Make disciples of all nations, baptizing them in the name of the Father, the Son and the Holy Spirit.

- God's initial instructions to Adam and Eve were to multiply, fill the earth, subdue it and rule over it. Through the authority of Christ, we are to make disciples of all nations, baptizing them in the name of the Lord and teaching them to do all that Christ commanded. These actions are intended to expand God's kingdom, ultimately bringing all things under its rule.

Summary

As we have examined the Word of God in light of what Jesus mission was, and we clearly see Jesus Christ mission was that of the Second Adam, restoring dominion back to humanity, and restoring humanity his mission. **Matthew 28:18-20;**

"And Jesus came and spake unto them, saying, All power is given unto me in heaven and in earth. ¹⁹Go ye therefore, and teach all nations, baptizing them in the name of the Father, and of the Son, and of the Holy Ghost: ²⁰Teaching them to observe all things whatsoever I have commanded you: and, lo, I am with you always, even unto the end of the world. Amen."

Chapter 2
Basic Training Part 1

Purpose

Spiritual warfare is a conflict between the devil and humankind, "Basic Training" of our preparation for spiritual warfare. In the previous section, we learned how our enemy, satan, opposes and attacks us in a variety of ways. *As God's adopted children through faith in Jesus Christ, we receive a commission in God's army to continue the work of Christ in bringing every enemy under Christ's authority.* With that in mind, we are given several instructions concerning readiness for battle.

What instructions concerning battle readiness does each of the following verses give us? We are to continue the mission of Jesus!

- Matthew 10:16; be wise as serpents and harmless as doves
- Ephesians 6:10, 11, 13; be strong in the Lord, put on the full
- Armor of God, stand firm against the devil's schemes, resists evil.
- James 4:7; Submit to God, resist the devil and he will flee Peter 5:8; Be of sober spirit & be on alert, because the enemy prowls around like a lion seeking who he may devour.

We can assume that our enemy is well skilled in warring against humanity and has about 6000 years of experience!

Training is an essential activity for the warriors who hope to succeed in resisting the enemy and advancing God's kingdom. In this section, we will explore some fundamental areas that we should be familiar with warfare, including the forces, their capabilities, and the enemy's typical tactics.

A. Kingdoms in Conflict

In conventional warfare, military intelligence is often a key ingredient to victory. In spiritual warriors, it is important for us to understand the two kingdoms in conflict and the relative capabilities of each.

I. The Kingdom God (Heavenly Father, God the Son, God the Holy Spirit)

A. Characteristics - Jesus used many parables to describe the characteristics of God's kingdom. In the following scripture passages here are some aspects of God's kingdom that is described in the Holy Bible.
- **Matthew 13:31-33**, Expanding may have small or insignificant beginning, but will grow to be large (mustard seed parable); spreads like yeast through dough.
- **Matthew 18:3-4**, James 4:6, Based on humility, pride has no part in it, and Childlike mankind determines entry and greatness in the kingdom.
- **Mark 16:17**, Philippians 2:9-11, Superior to satan kingdom.
- **Hebrews 13:8**, He is Everlasting
- **Hebrews 12:28**, He is Unshakeable

Jesus' many parables illustrated a kingdom that was radically different from earthly kingdoms. This difference is especially evident in the concept of greatness in the kingdom. In earthly kingdoms, military might, wealth and political power is typical measures of greatness. In God's kingdom, such things are foolishness, as God has unlimited power and resources. So how is greatness measured in his kingdom? From the following scripture passages, it shows how greatness is measured in God's kingdom:

- **Matthew 5:19;** Obedience to God
- **Matthew 18:3-4,** James 4:6; Humility
- **Matthew 20:25-28,** Matthew 23:11; Servant hood

B. The Commander-in-Chief

Read Ephesians 1:20-23 and Revelation 19:11-16.
Who is in command of God's army? Jesus.
Some of the names that he is known by are Faithful and True, the Word of God, and King of Kings and Lord of Lords

Description of Jesus The Christ – He looked like a shaft of light. He is so glorious. "Jesus is 5' 11" – 6'0 feet tall, Jesus is beautiful - not just but beautiful. His hair is light brown but appears to be white because of the glory of God that is emanating from Him. His eyes are like pools of love. When you look into His eyes you see love and kindness, He can look right through a person.

He can be looking at millions of people, yet you are the only one He has seen. His clothes are beautiful robes of various colors, which look like solid diamonds when they are sparkling, and a golden sash. His feet look like burnished brass, and there are holes in His hands and feet about the size of a nickel. There is a brilliance coming out of Him that seemed to be like waves of glory.

Love is permeating from him. Jesus is now seated in heaven in authority at the right hand of the Father, far above all evil principality, power, might, dominion and every name, *every foe of God belongs under the Authority of Christ.*

Angels.

Holy Angels are created spiritual beings that do God's bidding. God can give angels great power and authority to carry out missions (ex. Revelation 18:1).

Listed below are some of the typical missions angels are sent to do, along with an example from scriptures we have several verses, briefly summarize what happened.

1) Execute God's judgment on the earth

In 1 Chronicles 21:15-27; God sent an angel to destroy Jerusalem with a plague, other examples: Genesis 19:13, Numbers 22:22, 31-32. Serve in God's army, which may intervene in human conflicts. 2 Samuel 5:23-25; God's army assists David in defeating the Philistines, Other examples: 2 Kings 19:35, Joshua 5:136:5;

Fight against satan and his angels Daniel 10:11-13, 20; Gabriel and Michael fight the "princes" of Persia and Greece (i.e. evil angels). Another example: Revelation 12:7-9.

2) Help God's people

Helping God's people is an angelic role, particularly relevant to spiritual warfare. God's angels are "flames of fire" that minister to Christians (Hebrews 1:7, 14).

3) Give instructions

Angels have the ability to intervene in mans affairs.

In Daniel 8:15-27, Angel explains Daniel's vision of the end times, Acts 1:10-11; Two angels explain to the disciples that Jesus will return to earth. Other examples: Acts 10:22, Revelation 1:1. (Protect)

In 2 Kings 6:17, God's angelic army surrounded Elisha as "horses and chariots full of fire." Other examples: Psalm 34:7, Psalm 91:11-12.

4) Respond to prayer

In Daniel 10:12, the angel Gabriel responded to Daniel's prayer, Acts 12:5-11; Angel frees Peter from prison in response to Christians' prayers. Another example: Matthew 26:53.

5) Strengthen people

In Daniel 10:18-19; the angel touched Daniel and strengthened him, Matthew 4:11; the angels ministered to Jesus after the Devil finished tempting him. Another example: Luke 22:43.

We should remember that God directs the holy angels (Psalm 91:11), not us. We are to pray to God, not to the angels. Many non-Christian religions involve praying to deities who in fact are not gods, but demons or "fallen angels." (Ex. Deuteronomy 32:17).

6) People

People who believe and obey Jesus Christ are among the most effective troops in God's army.

Summary

Again, "Basic Training" is our preparation for spiritual warfare. In the previous section, we learned how our enemy, satan, opposes and attacks us in a variety of ways.

As God's adopted children through faith in Jesus Christ, *we receive a commission, and it is essential in God's army to continue the work of Christ in bringing every enemy under Christ's authority.* With that in mind, we are given several instructions concerning readiness for battle.

Chapter 3
Basic Training Part 2 Our identity in Christ

Purpose

Now that we have reviewed the origin of the spiritual conflict between the devil and humankind, we can begin the "Basic Training" of our preparation for spiritual warfare. In the previous section, we learned how our enemy, satan, opposes and attacks us in a variety of ways.

As God's adopted children through faith in Jesus Christ, we receive a commission in God's army to continue the work of Christ in bringing every enemy under Christ's authority. With that in mind, we are given several instructions concerning readiness for battle.

A. What is our identity in Christ?

In Galatians 4:7, a son of God and heir to his kingdom, and Philippians 3:20-21. We are citizens of heaven, awaiting transformation of our earthly bodies into heavenly ones.

In Reading Second Timothy 2:1-4, what is our role in God's army? As we are soldiers of Jesus Christ, and reading 1 John 4:4, whom do we have in us that is greater than satan? The Holy Spirit.

It is imperative that we know our identity in Christ, as understand that we are seated with Christ in heavenly place. We have been given power, and authority over the devil.

B. What are we commission to do?

Mark 16:15 "Go into all the world and preach the gospel to every creature."

Acts 1:8, The Holy Spirit empowered witnesses for Christ in the world.

As a born, again believer, YOUR POSITION IN CHRIST, and when negative or tormenting thoughts begin to bombard your mind. You need to "take these thoughts captive by replacing them with truth."

1 John 4:4 *"Ye are of God, little children, and have overcome them: because greater is he that is in you, than he that is in the world."*

The Holy Spirit abide within the born-again believers new created spirit.

- I renounce the lie that I am rejected, unloved, dirty or shameful because in Christ
- I am completely accepted. God says that…
- I am God's child (John 1:12) I have been adopted into the family of God
- (Ephesians 1:5)
- I am Christ's friend (John 15:15), I have been justified (Romans 5:1)
- I am united with the Lord, and I am one spirit with Him (1 Corinthians 6:17)
- I have been bought with a price; I belong to God (1 Corinthians 6:19, 20)
- I am a member of Christ's body (1 Corinthians 12:27)
- I am a saint, a holy one (Ephesians 1:1)

- I have direct access to God through the Holy Spirit (Ephesians 2:8)
- I have been redeemed and forgiven of all my sins (Colossians 1:4; 1John 1:9)
- I am complete in Christ (Colossians 2:10)
- I am free forever from condemnation (Romans 8:1, 2)

The Holy Spirit convicts - the devil condemns, Conviction is not condemnation

- I am assured that all things work together for good (Romans 8:28)
- I am free from any condemning against me (Romans 8:31-34)
- I cannot be separated from the love of God (Romans 8:35-39)
- I have been established, anointed and sealed by God (2 Corinthians 1:21, 22)
- I am confident that He who has begun in me will complete it (Philippians 1:6)
- I am a citizen of heaven (Philippians 3:20)
- I am hidden with Christ in God (Colossians 3:3)
- I have not been given a spirit of fear, but of power, love and a sound mind (2 Timothy 1:7)
- I can find grace and mercy to help in time of need (Hebrews 4:16)
- I am born of God, and the evil one cannot touch me (1 John 5:18) [Though I am not exempt from spiritual warfare]

- I renounce the lie that I am worthless, inadequate, helpless or Hopeless because in Christ I am deeply significant. God says **that...**
- I am the salt of the earth and the light of the world (Matthew 5:13, 14)
- I am a branch of the true vine, Jesus, a channel of His life (John 15:1, 5)
- I have been chosen and appointed by God to bear fruit (John 15:16)
- I am a personal, Spirit-empowered witness of Christ's (Acts 1:8)
- I am a temple of God (1 Corinthians 3:16)
- I am a minister of reconciliation for God (2 Corinthians 5:17-21)
- I am God's coworker (2 Corinthians 6:1)
- I am seated with Christ in the heavenly realm (Ephesians 2:6)
- I am God's workmanship, created for good works (Ephesians 2:10)
- I may approach God with freedom and confidence (Ephesians 3:12)
- I can do all things through Christ who strengthens me! (Philippians 4:13)
- I am not the great "I am," but by the grace of God I am what I am.
- (Exodus 3:14, John 8:24, 28, 58, 1 Corinthians 15:10).

Summary

God wants us to know beyond all shadow of a doubt about how secure we are in Him. Knowing how secure, we are in Him is not a license to continue in our sin, but instead letting that security be the fuel that kindles the fire of determination inside us allowing God to break any stronghold(s) of sin in our lives.

Bare also in mind: Our uncrucified area of flesh delights in working in concert with the devil, and we cannot cast full blame on the devil every time we sin. The devil usually tempts us in the areas of the flesh, where we are the weakest. As children of God, we will be rewarded at the Judgment Seat of Christ for setting our standards as high as God has set them in His Word.

It is easy to apply 1 John 1:9 every time we sin and keep sinning the same sin repeatedly and asking forgiveness for it year after year, time after time.

Sexual sins especially come to mind, of the "personal" nature. God wants us calling sin ... "SIN" ... criminal acts against God's laws, which are criminal acts against God Himself and putting to death every sin we keep committing. When we raise our standards of holiness of what we will tolerate in our lives and what we want, it is incredible the power God gives us to gain victory over temptations of sin we have not been able to gain victory over previously.

Chapter 4
The Armor of God Introduction

One of the greatest lies that satan seeks to do is blind Christians to the fact is that 'They have no spiritual battle.' When Christians do not believe they are in a battle, they will not use their spiritual weapons to fight the devil, and this is precisely WHY the devil does all he can to try to keep Christians blind to his influence over them." If Christians do not believe there is a battle in the spiritual realm, they will depend on their academic knowledge and live a defeated life.

God wants you and I to recognize an attack… then learn how to stay one-step ahead of satan attacks against us as much as possible. So that when he attacks (not if he attacks), we will have the wisdom to know it is a demonic attack.

We will purpose to walk ever closer to the Lord in trusting Him to reveal to us how to cooperate with the Lord to demonstrate satan defeat. *"Wherefore take unto you the whole armor of God that ye may be able to withstand in the evil day, and having done all, to stand"* Ephesians 6:13.

Spiritually Dressed for Success

A. The Belt of Truth

Ephesians 6:13-14 *"Therefore, take up the full armor of God, so that you will be able to resist in the evil day, and having done everything, to stand firm" "Be of sober spirit, be on the alert your adversary, the devil, prowls around like a roaring lion, seeking someone to devour"*

1 Peter 5:8 *"Be sober, be vigilant, because you adversary the devil, as a roaring lion, walketh about, seeking whom he may devour."*

James 4:7 *"Submit therefore to God. Resist the devil and he will flee from you"* **John 8:32** *"Ye shall know the truth"*

Hosea 4:6 *"My people are destroyed for lack of knowledge: because thou hast rejected knowledge, I will also reject thee, that thou shalt be no priest to me: seeing thou hast forgotten the law of thy God, I will also forget thy children"*

The belt that girds it all securely together and demonstrates the believer's readiness for war is the truth. Alethia, translated "truth," refers to the content of that which is true. One aspect of truth is the content of God's Word, which is essential for the believer in his battle against the schemes of the devil.

Without the truth of Scripture, as the apostle has already pointed out, we are subject to being "carried about by every wind of doctrine, by the trickery of men, by craftiness in deceitful scheming" Ephesians 4:14. "New world order religion Chris lam."

B. The Breast Plate of Righteousness

Ephesians 6:14. "Stand firm therefore, having girded your loins with truth, and having put on the breastplate of righteousness"

The purpose of that piece of armor is obvious—to protect the heart, lungs, intestines, and other vital organs. The breastplate of righteousness that we put on, as a part spiritual armor against our adversary is the practical righteousness of a life lived in obedience to God's Word.

It is the moral behavior of the believer as found in Ephesians 4:24-27, which having been done, will "not give the devil opportunity" Colossians 3:9-14. 2 Corinthians 1:30, 5:21.

The breastplate is then put on to protect men and help believers in righteousness and along with the belt. This armor is never to be removed.

No Roman soldier would go into battle without his breastplate, a tight, sleeveless piece of armor that covered his full torso. It was often made of leather or heavy linen, onto which were sewn overlapping slices of animal hooves or horns or pieces of metal. Some were made of large pieces of metal molded or hammered to conform to the body.

C. The Shoes of the Gospel of Peace

Ephesians 6:15 "... And having shod your feet with the preparation of the gospel of peace..."

The purpose of shoes (boots) allows the soldier to be ready to march, climb, fight, or do whatever else is necessary. It is not a fashion statement. Roman soldier's shoes had a much different purpose, then the shoes you may have on because a soldier's very life could depend on them.

As he marches on rough hot roads, climbs over jagged rocks, tramples over thorns, and wades through streambeds of jagged stones, his feet will need much protection.

A soldier whose feet is blistered, cut or swollen cannot fight well and often is not even able to stand up to the perilous situation in battle. A Christian's spiritual footwear is equally important. Verse 15 says, "And your feet shod with the preparation of the gospel of peace." The Greek word for preparation has the general meaning of readiness.

D. The Shield of Faith

Ephesians 6:16; "In addition to all, taking up the shield of faith with which you will be able to extinguish all the flaming arrows of the evil one"

• A shield can be a very threatening thing. I cannot think of a shield that has flowers on it or a happy face. Most shields have emblems on them that invoke fear. An army that is advancing wants to strike fear into the hearts of their enemy. Fear can be very damaging.

• Paul explains the need to be equipped with the shield of faith. He has a break here in the list of armor. "In addition to all" introduces the last three pieces of armor.

• The first three, the belt, breastplate, and shoes were for the long-range preparation and protection and were never taken off on the battlefield.

The shield, helmet, and sword, on the other hand, were kept in readiness for use when actual fighting began.

1 John 5:4 "For whatever is born of God overcomes the world; and this is the victory that has overcome the world our faith."

> *"Every word of God is tested; He is a shield to those who take refuge in Him. Do not add to His words or He will reprove you, and you will be proved a liar."* **Proverbs 30:5-6**

- The soldiers who carried these shields were in the front lines of battle and usually stood side by side with their shields together, forming a horizontal wall extending as long as a mile or more.
- This kind of a stance would strike fear in the enemy because from a distance it was hard to see where the break was. It looked like a solid wall.
- The shields were also used in the aerial attack.
- The archers stood behind this protective wall of shields and shot their arrows as they advanced against the enemy. Anyone who stood or crouched behind such shields was protected from the barrage of enemy arrows and spears. The shield, which had a covering of metal or leather soaked in water, was the most reliable protection against such flaming missiles because would either deflect or extinguish them.
- The devil continually bombards God's children with temptations to immorality, hatred, envy, anger, covetousness, pride, doubt, fear, despair, distrust, and every other sin. These sound like fiery missiles to me.

The initial devil temptation of Adam and Eve was to entice them to doubt God and instead to put their trust in his lies. The first of his flaming missiles, from which all the others have lighted their flames, every temptation, directly or indirectly, is the temptation to doubt and distrust God.

E. The Helmet of Salvation

Ephesians 6:17
"And take the helmet of salvation, and the sword of the Spirit, which is the word of God".

1 Thessalonians 5:8.

"But since we are of the day, let us be sober, having put on the breastplate of faith and love, and as a helmet, the hope of salvation."

The purpose of the Helmet of salvation is to prevent head injuries, because head injuries are a serious issue.

There have been accidents where victims had what seemed to be minor injuries, but because there was a blow to the head, they had serious head trauma. Even people riding bicycles can have serious head injuries if they fall. Think about it. Would you want to play professional football with no helmet? That is why we need this protection. The devil has a double-edged sword that he attacks the believer with discouragement when he points to our failures, our sins, and our unresolved problems.

Our poor health, or to whatever else seems negative in our lives in order to make us lose confidence in the love and care of our heavenly Father. Doubt is designed to separate us from truly knowing and following Christ wholeheartedly.

Doubt is the very reason why a person has trouble-knowing God more, through prayer and scripture.

We may be tempted to doubt our calling. Our choice of a marriage partner, our job, our abilities, and so many other things. Doubt has a tendency to cripple us just as a head injury may cripple someone who otherwise is perfectly healthy.

F. Sword of the Spirit

Ephesians 6:17 "And take the helmet of salvation, and the sword of the Spirit, which is the word of God"

Hebrews 4:12 "For the word of God is living and active and sharper than any two-edged sword, and piercing as far as the division of soul and spirit, of both joints and marrow, and able to judge the thoughts and intentions of the heart"

The other parts of his armor are meant to withstand the attacks of the enemy, but the weapon he carries is meant to attack, to strew down those that stand before him. I am sure a shield can become a weapon but not nearly as useful as a sword or gun. A weapon can shout death and defeat to those who come against it. It brings this sense of fear because of the more significant the weapon, the greater the fall.

Why is it then that believer should put on the whole armor, except for their swords? Those that do pick up the sword are not sure how to use it or may even cut themselves before they are a threat to the enemy.

Paul says that our weapon is the sword of the Spirit, which is the Word of God. This type of sword could be pulled out quickly and thrust into the enemy when under attack.

The more familiar we are with the weapon, the better equipped we are to use it correctly and the better equipped we are in keeping it in good working condition and keeping ourselves safe.

The Holy Spirit is our helper and trainer, and He will teach us and help us to remember what we have been taught. Others can help us in this training as well, although the Holy Spirit is our top trainer. We can call upon friends, pastors, and family members to help us in this training.

How to practice the use of Scripture:

>**(1)** Read God's Word,
>**(2)** Know God's Word,
>**(3)** Meditate on God's Word,
>**(4)** Hide God's Word in your heart.

When we pick up the sword of the Spirit, we become on offensive soldier. We will be able to:

Expose deeds of darkness through The Word of God is a light, which will shine out in the darkness and expose all that is in it. Ephesians 5:13; Psalm 119:105, 130.

We can refute worldly philosophies and false religions – God's Word is truth and will refute the false claims and the misguided, James 5:19-20.

Preach the Gospel of Salvation; the greatest way that we can damage the kingdom of satan is to turn people away from satan to Christ Jesus through the Gospel.

2 Timothy 3:16-17 "All Scripture is inspired by God and profitable for teaching, for reproof, for correction, for training in righteousness, so that the man of God may be adequate, equipped for every good work".

G. Praying through the Armor of God with all prayers

Ephesians 6:13 "Therefore, take up the full armor of God, so that you will be able to resist in the evil day, and having done everything, to stand firm"

We are called to put on the armor of God. It is only then that we will be able to stand up against the onslaught that satan has for us each day. I do not think there is one of us who would want to be plopped down in the middle of a battle with no armor. The devil will come against us in a multitude of ways:

Undermining - God's character and credibility,
Persecution - peer pressure, or peaceful preoccupation,
Confusing - the believer with false doctrine,
Hindering - the believer's service to Christ,
Causing - division in the Body of Christ,
Urging - believers trust their own resources,
Causing - the believer to be hypercritical,
Making - believers worldly; and causing - us to disobey God's Word.

Although it is very important to be aware of the devices of satan, our defense against them is not simply our knowledge of them.

The armor has been provided for the daily battle. We can be equipped with this armor through the power of prayer.

Putting on Jesus

*When we put on the Armor of God, we are putting on the Lord Jesus Christ, can you see the wonderful provision of God that we have in Christ. For instance, **Number 1**, we have the belt of truth. Jesus said He is the truth (See John 14:6). **Number 2**, we have the breastplate of righteousness, and the Bible says that Jesus has been made unto us <u>our righteousness</u> (See 1 Corinthians 1:30). **Number 3**, we are to wear the shoes of the gospel of peace, and we read that Jesus Himself is <u>our peace</u> (See Ephesians 2:14). **Number 4**, we have the shield of faith, and the Bible says that Jesus is the author and the perfect of our faith (See Hebrews 12:2). **Number 5**, we have the helmet of salvation, and Jesus' title is Savior (See John 1:1). **Number 6**, we have the sword of the spirit, the word of God (See Hebrews 12:2). **Number 7**, we get Dress to Pray*

PRAY IN THE SPIRIT and intercede for all Christians as the Holy Spirit prompts me. I believe that the Holy Spirit is interceding on my behalf, according to my prayers.

Jude 20; *"But ye, beloved, building up yourselves on your most holy faith, praying in the Holy Ghost,"*

James 5:14-16; *"Is any sick among you? Let him call for the elders of the church; and let them pray over him, anointing him with oil in the name of the Lord: 15And the prayer of faith shall save the sick, and the Lord shall raise him up; and if he has committed sins, they shall be forgiven him. 16Confess your faults one to another, and pray one for another, that ye may be healed. The effectual fervent prayer of a righteous man availeth much.*

Romans 8:26-28, *"Likewise the Spirit also helpeth our infirmities: for we know not what we should pray for as we ought: but the Spirit itself maketh intercession for us with groanings which cannot be uttered. ²⁷And he that searcheth the hearts knoweth what is the mind of the Spirit, because he maketh intercession for the saints according to the will of God. ²⁸And we know that all things work together for good to them that love God, to them who are the called according to his purpose.*

Heavenly Father, I come afresh today ___/__/___ I surrender my spirit, soul "mind, will, emotions, imagination", I present my body, my sensory mechanism to YOU, I lay my life on the altar of consecration before YOU. Heavenly Father, I come thanking you for your word, and for the leading of the Holy Spirit, desiring that you will be down in my life. I want to, be like my Lord and Savior who lived a life in daily intimacy of closeness and in constant fellowship with You.

Heavenly Father, I want to know your will more clearly, with absolute certainty of divine guidance with instructions on not only what to do, but to how to do it. Heavenly Father, work in me to do YOUR will, and to do YOUR good pleasure because for that purpose I am here in the earth only to do your will. Heavenly Father, you are Almighty God "El-Elyon," the Most High, I bless and praise you in Jesus name, Amen.

Chapter 5
Warfare Disciplines

Purpose

In this section, we will examine disciplines that will help us in combat. Conventional military armies typically spend much time training in the various skill areas needed to fight wars. In this fashion, they are best prepared to face potential threats when war comes. Similarly, spiritual warriors can train in key skill areas, i.e., warfare disciplines, so that they are prepared to face the enemy when he attacks. We know that we are already at war and the devil is prowling around like a lion, looking for whom he may devour (1Peter 5:8).

When we are trained in the various disciplines needed to fight him, we will be better prepared for his attacks.

Our Trainer and trainers:

(1) God as the Master Trainer - As with most disciplines, it makes sense to be trained by a master. *God is the Master Trainer in spiritual warfare and works through the "person" of the Holy Spirit.*

Read Psalm 18:28-39, who trained David how to fight the enemy? God. What was David specially trained to do? - God taught his hands to make war (vs. 34). How was David equipped for battle? - God armed him with strength, agility, firm footing, strategic positioning, vision, and protection. God will provide all of the equipment we need, so that we may stand against the devil's schemes to survive and overcome!

Who trained Jesus and prepared him to face the devil in spiritual warfare? Luke 3:21-23, 4:1-2, the Holy Spirit. How did Jesus prove his own expertise in spiritual warfare? Hebrews 4:14-16, He was tempted in every way that we are, but did not sin.

Who has God sent to live in us and act as a counselor\train us? John 14:15-18, 1 John 4:4, the Spirit of Truth (the Holy Spirit).

What will the Holy Spirit do for us? How can this help us in spiritual warfare? John 14:26, 1 John 2:27, Help us, train us, and remind us of Christ's words.

He will also give us an "anointing" that will help us learn spiritual things, such as using spiritual weapons. For example, by reminding us of Christ's words, the Holy Spirit helps us to utilize the Sword of the Spirit with greater accuracy.

(2) People as Trainers

God, will also work through godly people in our lives to facilitate our warfare training. While these people are not our "masters," they can be agents of The Master in our lives. In the following verses, what people are mentioning are they who could be involved in our spiritual training?

Read Ephesians 4:11-12, Apostles, prophets, evangelists, teachers, pastors. Read first Corinthians 4:14-16, Spiritual fathers, and mentors. Read 1 Corinthians 12:2728, Apostles, prophets, teachers, people with gifts of miracles, healings, helps, administrations and various kinds of tongues.

Where are we most likely to find people who can train us? Acts 13:1, 1 Corinthians 12:28, in the church, with that in mind, what does the scriptures exhort us to continue doing?

Read Hebrews 10:23-26, Hold fast to our confession of faith without wavering, consider how to encourage one another to love and good deeds, and continue meeting together with other Christians for mutual encouragement in the faith.

Considering the above verses from Hebrews 10, how can you be involved with a church help you when you fail or get discouraged in warfare? Being part of a church body affords us the benefits of the various ministries of the people in the church. For example, if we are discouraged, we can be encouraged by people in the church. If we are struggling with doubt, we can benefit from someone with the gift of faith in the church. If we are feeling spiritually lazy, people who are zealous for the Lord can stir us to action.

(3) Disciplines to promote combat readiness - In this section, we will look at five disciplines that will help us in fighting spiritual warfare battles.

Mastering these disciplines will contribute to increasing your endurance on the battlefield. Besides, recognize the enemy's schemes; be effective in response to the battle, and sharper discernment of God's guidance.

A. Quiet times

Military units typically muster in the morning each day for several reasons.

The commanding officer needs an accurate account of his forces, and the forces need their orders for the day's evolutions. The commanding officer may use this time to communicate with his soldiers on pertinent matters, such as providing praise, rebuke, warning, guidance, encouragement. He may brief the soldiers on the latest intelligence reports and explain how that might affect the unit.

The soldiers may brief the commanding officer on essential developments in the field that could affect the unit's combat readiness. The morning muster is critical to the unit's mission accomplishment for that particular day. Likewise, it is crucial for us to meet with God, our commanding officer, each day for us to meet our mission objectives in spiritual warfare.

Though, not a difficult task, it can be a big challenge for people to have a quiet time consistently merely. The cares of the world, lack of sleep, or busy schedules so often vie for priority over time with God. If we hope to be valiant warriors in God's army, we cannot afford to miss our daily quiet time with Him!

What happens when we fail to connect with God? John 15:4, we are separated from the vine (Christ) and cannot bear fruit for his kingdom. Read Psalm 63, what was the condition of David's soul and body (while being chased by Saul in the wilderness)? David's soul longed for the Lord; his flesh thirsted for the Lord. What did he do in response? David sought the Lord early in the morning and worshiped him. What were the results?

His soul was satisfied, and he rejoiced as God upheld him with His right hand; his enemies were (to be) destroyed, the liars' mouths were (to be) stopped.

Quiet times can be a strategic time for us to seek God's wisdom about the challenges we are facing in the natural or spiritual realms.

In reading Joshua 9:1-19 what, did Joshua and the elders fail to do? Joshua and the elders did not seek the Lord about the proposed peace treaty with the strangers. What happened as a result? As a result, they were deceived and made a treaty with the very people God had instructed them to remove from the land.

1. Elements of meaningful quiet times - There is perhaps an unlimited number of things we can do in our quiet times. What matters most is the condition of our heart.

Please read each verse reference and write down the quiet time activity mentioned. Read Joshua 1:8, Bible study (scripture study, meditation, and memory work) Read Psalm 100:4, Praise & Worship; Read Ephesians 6:10-13, Put on the full armor of God and Read Ephesians 6:18 "Prayer."

A. Testing doctrine, spirits and people

The devil often uses false doctrine, deceiving spirits and people to divide churches and lead people away from Christ. If we plan to survive and be victorious in spiritual warfare, we will need to develop the skills of testing doctrine, spirits, and people. God's word is the most important source we can study to recognize the various counterfeits that the devil uses.

How relevant or useful is God's word to the challenges that we face in life? Read 2 Timothy 3:16-17, the scriptures are perfectly relevant and useful. All scripture is profitable for doctrine, reproof, correction, and training in righteousness, this directly contributes to our readiness for warfare and the fulfillment of God's mission for our lives.

What were the key phrases that Paul used to describe God's word in Hebrews 4:12? Living and active, sharper than any two-edged sword, Pierces even to the division of soul and spirit, and of joints and marrow, is a discerner of the thoughts and intents of the heart.

How did Jesus use the word of God to fight satan temptations? Jesus used the word to expose and refute satan temptations. Jesus quoted the scriptures that revealed satan true motives.

If Jesus had not known the scriptures, how might the outcome of this confrontation be different? Had he not known the scriptures, Jesus may have succumbed to any of satan three temptations.

How did the Bereans test the apostles' teaching? Read Acts 17:10-12, they searched the scriptures to see if what the apostles were saying was correct. The scriptures help us recognize satan, his minions, and his schemes, typically by the fruits they produce.

Jesus said, "A good tree bringeth not forth corrupt fruit; neither doth a corrupt tree brings forth good fruit. For every tree is known by his own fruit. For of thorns, men do not gather figs, nor of a bramble bush gather the grapes" (Luke 6:43-44).

Please see the list of the fruits (or qualities) of the false prophets that Peter recognized/described. Read 2 Peter 2:1-19, denying the Lord, follow wicked ways and bring the way of truth into disrepute. Greedy and exploitive, follow the corrupt desire of the sinful nature and despise authority; bold & arrogant; blasphemous; like brute beasts; revealed in their pleasures; Eyes full of adultery, and they never stop sinning; seduce the unstable; land over the wages of wickedness.

B. Controlling our thoughts

Controlling our thoughts could be the most difficult discipline to master in spiritual warfare. It is particularly tricky because three different sources can feed evil thoughts into our minds. What are the three sources of evil thoughts mentioned in the below verses?

Matthew 15:18-20; The Heart; Matthew 16:21-23; People; and Acts 5:3; the devil.

Psalm 66:18, Blocked prayer: "If I regard iniquity in my heart, the Lord will not hear me"

C. Exercising Godliness please read 2 Peter 1:3-7.

1. **Physical & Spiritual exercise compared** – Any exercise involves working against resistance. For example, weightlifters' resistance consists of the weight on the barbell or dumbbell. A swimmer's resistance comes from the friction or drag of their bodies moving through the water. Overcoming the resistance is the work that breaks the muscles down so that they will grow stronger.

The same principles of resistance and strength building apply in spiritual exercise.

What is the internal resistance we face in exercising godliness? Read Romans 7:21-25, the law of sin in our members' wars against the law of our minds (God's laws). What did Paul instruct Timothy to do regarding godliness? Read 1 Timothy 4:6-eight. Exercise himself toward godliness. What did Paul liken spiritual training too? Physical training (or exercise)

In what way is a spiritual exercise superior to physical exercise? Read 1 Corinthians 9:24-27, it is profitable for all things, both now and eternity. Paul used the comparison of physical training to illustrate spiritual training principles here, just as he did in 1 Timothy 4:6-8.

What two recommendations did Paul have for spiritual athletes, drawing from his own experience with spiritual training? Most athletes who want to improve their skill level beyond their own knowledge invest in a trainer.

Run to get the prize, i.e., take it seriously and keep the eternal reward in mind. Be prepared to exercise self-control in everything. Paul disciplined his body and brought it under strict control so that he would not be "disqualified" from the race.

What did Paul have to bring into submission during his spiritual training? What was at stake if he failed to do so? His flesh, he could be disqualified from his inheritance in Christ (the eternal prize).

The race analogy of the Christian life emphasizes the ongoing battle we must fight against our flesh. The body is continually gravitating toward sin and will resist yielding to the desires of the Holy Spirit.

Paul struggled with this ongoing war, as reflected in Romans 7:14-25. Thankfully, God has given us power through the Holy Spirit to overcome the slavery of sin (and the flesh) and to bring our bodies into obedience to God.

2. **Examples of how to exercise godliness** - What does it mean to exercise godliness? Scripture describes many practical ways to exercise godliness. For each of the eight examples below, please complete the statement and then see what the passage says concerning that way of exercising godliness. We exercise godliness by presenting our bodies as living sacrifices. Romans 12:1-2.

A. Prayer is the Christians lifeline

It is an open communication link with God. It seems that human nature gravitates away from God. Reverting to self-reliance through practical solutions to the daily challenges, we face. It is all too easy to forget God while trying to do things on our own. This is actually a form of pride that we must resist if we hope to grow in our relationship with God and be fruitful for his kingdom.

Prayer helps us be in tune with God. It can open our eyes and ears to sense where he is working in the situations around us.

For spiritual warfare, prayer is the battle communication link that gives us important and possibly life-saving info to help us fight the enemy.

If we can master the skill of continuous prayer, we will be more effective in spiritual warfare and more efficient as an agent of God's kingdom. Continuous prayer is like an open dialogue with God throughout the day, whether spoken or in our thoughts. It is where we share our feelings, concerns, thoughts, and dreams with God.

1. The strategic importance of prayer – Read Philippians 4:6-7. What instructions did Paul give concerning the challenges of life and prayer? Do not be anxious about anything; take everything to God with prayer and supplication.

2. The frequency of prayer – Read 1 Thessalonians 5:16-18, what did Paul say about the frequency of prayer? Pray without ceasing. What two things did Paul mention that could be done in conjunction with prayer? Rejoice always and in everything give thanks.

3. Persistence in Prayer – Read Luke 11:5-13, why did the man in the house give his friend the food? Because of his persistence. How did Jesus apply this to prayer? Jesus used the parable of the persistent friend to show how we should be persistent in prayer (ask, seek, knock) because it will yield results.

4. Examples - The scriptures give us plenty of examples of people praying. The examples below illustrate the variety of situations that people prayed in the Bible.

Please read the verses below and describe the occasions that prayers were offered. Read Mark 1:29-39.

Jesus takes time out to pray early in the morning just as his healing ministry is getting started, He is in high demand, yet takes time to pray. (See Acts 1:12-14) The disciples and others were joined together regularly in prayer after the resurrection (See Acts 2:41-43).

The new believers continued steadfastly in doctrine, fellowship, breaking of bread and prayers results: "fear came upon every soul, and many wonders and signs were done through the apostles."

(See Acts 6:3-5) The apostles appointed overseers, to the ministry so that they could devote themselves continually to preaching and prayer.

(See Acts 10:1-23) Cornelius was a devout man who feared God, gave alms to the poor generously and prayed always. An angel appeared to him during prayer and instructed him to send men to find Peter.

Peter was praying on the rooftop and had a vision, the Holy Spirit, then told him to go with the men that Cornelius had sent. The critical meeting of Cornelius and Peter (which resulted in the Gentiles receiving the Holy Spirit) was arranged through prayer. (See Acts 16:24-26) Paul and Silas were praising God and praying at midnight in prison. Looking at your own prayer life, what are the typical times that you pray?

Summary

Spiritual warfare, as God's adopted children through faith in Jesus Christ; we receive a commission in God's army to continue the work of Christ in bringing every enemy under Christ's authority. With that in mind, we are given several instructions concerning readiness for battle. People who believe and obey Jesus Christ are among the most effective troops in God's army.

- The one thing that we must master to become an effective spiritual warrior is to love others.
- The second essential for spiritual warfare preparedness is Belief and obedience to Christ.

Chapter 6
Exposing the Kingdom of Darkness

Purpose

Now that we have reviewed the origin of the spiritual conflict between good and evil, we can begin the "Basic Training" of our preparation for spiritual warfare. In the previous section, we learned how our enemy, satan, opposes and attacks us in a variety of ways. We God's adopted children through faith in Jesus Christ.

We receive a commission in God's army to continue the work of Christ in bringing every enemy under Christ's authority. With that in mind, we are given several instructions concerning readiness for battle.

A. The kingdom of Darkness (devil)

1. Characteristics - satan kingdom is opposed to God's kingdom in every way. In the following scriptures, the verses reveal the characteristic of satan kingdom that is illustrated: Daniel 10:13, 20, satan kingdom is in rebellion against God; Revelation 20:10, 14, satan has a temporary kingdom, and Matthew 12:24-30, Inferior to God's Kingdom Jesus demonstrated this by casting demons out.

B. The Commander and Chief

As we studied previously, satan was formerly the angel, lucifer (Isaiah 14:12), who was the covering cherub for God's throne (Ezekiel 28:12-16).

He is the current ruler of the earth (Luke 4:5-6, John 12:31) and is referred to as the "prince of the power of the air, the spirit who now works in the sons of disobedience" (Ephesians 2:2 NKJV). He is the "Father of Lies" (John 8:44), He has authority, power and a throne (Revelation 13:2); He will ultimately give his throne, his power, and authority to the beast (Revelation 13:2).

1. Description of satan / beelzebub - "His head is large and dark, and he looked like a man, yet at the same time, like some kind of animal or grotesque creature that is beyond description. Upon his head, he wears a silver crown, from his temple on both sides there are two long white tapeworms, and they move in every direction. He has two big, red eyes, shaped like the eyes of a serpent.

He is broad-chested, and his ribcage appeared to be constructed of pipes, his lower torso is cover with what looked like glass or diamonds, their color was red, purple, blue and green. He wears a black coat or cape, jet black.

The black coat or cape at first appearance may look like velvet, but it is really made up of files, maggots, and worms, and the smell, the odor that comes from his body is unbearable."

He has the power to change from time to time his appearance into an angel of light, but his most common appearance is an animal or grotesque, the most hideous form that you have ever seen, and evil and hatred permeate from him."

2. Forces - satan has a well-organized group of forces to carry out his schemes on the earth. With the exception of people who serve his purposes as satan forces are spiritual entities. In reading Ephesians 6:12, what are the various groups of evil forces under satan control? satan forces include principalities, powers, rulers of the darkness of this age, spiritual hosts of wickedness in the heavenly places. Who are these forces "wrestling" with us (Christians)!

C. Evil Angels - satan angels are involved in cosmic and human events, just as God's angels are. Scripture suggests the number of satan angels is one-third of God's original population of angels in (Revelation 12:3-9). Since there are "myriads and myriads" of God's angels, it follows that there is a large number of evil angels as well (Hebrews 12:22, Revelation 5:11).

1. Description of Demons and evil spirits: From the book Placebo by Howard Pitman, he shared the tour that was given to by the Angels that was escorting from the earth through the Second Heaven on His way to the Third Heaven. [5]

- The First most powerful type demon revealed to me was also in human form and these demons looked like ordinary people. All of the warring demons were colored bronze."

Appearing to be about eight to twelve feet tall, they were rugged and handsomely constructed, somewhat like giant athletes.

- The Second most powerful type and a group of demons were revealed to me in mixed shapes and forms.
- When we got down to the Third group, or orders, all the demons of this rank were revealed in forms other than human.
- The fourth group of demons – no detail
- Fifth group particular demons are harder to deal with than any of the rest. It seems their great strength rests in their ability to remain anonymous in their work in the human being.

2. Responses to spiritual warfare - As we have seen in previous examples, demons resist being expelled in a variety of ways. One of the reasons for this is that they apparently vary in power level. Let us examine another example, which illustrates this. Based on Mark 9:17-29, what did the spirit do when it saw Jesus?

Why do you think it did this? It immediately threw the boy into a convulsion.

3. People - People can knowingly or unknowingly further the plans of satan by doing evil. In reading Matthew 13:24-30, 36-43, what two groups of people does Jesus describe in this parable? Sons of God (the good seed) and sons of the wicked one.

4. How the enemy attacks us - The devil uses many tactics to accomplish his mission. By studying examples of the devil's tactics from scripture, we can better recognize them when we face them in spiritual warfare.

5. Tempt through the lust of the eyes, the lust of the flesh and pride of life. Tempting through lust and pride are perhaps the more obvious ways that satan and his Forces attack us. For each verse below, write down a short description of the temptations used: Genesis 3:1-6, Proverbs 6:23-28, Acts 5:3, 1 Timothy 6:9-10.

6. Steal, Kill and Destroy (John 10:10 NKJV) - In teaching about the Good Shepherd, Jesus contrasted himself with false shepherds who were thieves said, "The thief does not come except to steal, and to kill, and to destroy. I have come that they may have life and that they may have it more abundantly" Job 1:912, Matthew 13:19.

7. Oppose the Gospel of Christ - Another way the enemy attacks are by opposing the Gospel of Christ. satan opposes the Gospel to stop it from strengthening and expanding God's kingdom. One of thing believers must always be mindful is that satan opposed the Kingdom of God in every way.

Let us examine some examples of his opposition to the Gospel.

8. Veil the mind from the truth - One tactic that is particularly effective in warfare is to veil or blind the mind from the truth. satan has notable power to deceive people, i.e., to influence what people see and believe. Let us look at some examples of this "mind control" in the scriptures. (2 Corinthians 4:3-4, 2 Thessalonians 2:9-10.)

9. Weaken faith in God - Our faith is potentially a very powerful weapon against the enemy. When we believe God and his word, all things are possible to us.

It makes sense therefore that one of satan strategies is to weaken our faith in God. He does this in a variety of ways. Genesis 3:1-6, Luke 4:3; 9-12.

D. What are the snares of satan?

The devil may not always be present in a given temptation. He will use circumstances and human agents to accomplish his purposes. Ultimately, he will be the one at work behind the scenes. As the saying goes, "Behind the lie is the liar; behind the trap is the trapper."

1. **Greed** – Greed is a key snare and illustrates what is in the heart. In the movie Wall Street, Michael Douglas plays Gordon Gekko, who lauds the value of greed. Exodus 20:17, Proverbs 3:31, Galatians 5:21.

2. **Gambling** - Gambling affects not only the gambler but also those around him or her. In a sense, this snare arises from some other snares (greed, covetousness) it also surfaces because we are dissatisfied with God's provision.

3. **Alcoholism** - Alcoholism is a significant source of family disruption and economic devastation, as is an addiction to drugs. "The alcoholic must realize that something else is controlling him or her. The Bible teaches that we should not "get drunk with wine... but be filled with the Spirit" (Ephesians 5:1).

4. Pornography - Pornography not only can control our lives, but it also defiles our spirit. The Bible admonishes us to abstain from sinful desires (1 Peter 2:11) that war against our soul. Instead, we should live exemplary lives before the watching world (1 Peter 2:12).

5. Sexual Affairs - We live in a world of sexual freedom, and we hear false messages from the media and our culture, convincing us that happiness is just around the corner with the next sexual partner we meet. This is the myth of greener grass on the other side of the fence. Marriage should be "held in honor among all"(Hebrews 13:4). We are not to unite our bodies with another in sexual immorality (1 Corinthians 6:15-16).

6. The Search for Pleasure - We live in a society full of lovers of pleasure rather than lovers of God 2 Timothy 3:1-5.

7. Occultism - Movies and television shows promote the occult and make the dark side of evil look enticing, warn us to avoid the occult Deuteronomy 18:914.

8. Attitudes - We can lose altitude in the spirit with wrong attitudes toward the things of God. "Your attitude determines the altitude at which you soar in life." We can certainly see this truth. (See Deuteronomy 28:47, 48).

We can learn from this verse that even though we belong to the Lord if we do not serve Him with the right attitude of joy we can open up the door to the devil. When we have wrong attitudes, we lower our altitudes and descend within satan range of power!

The apostle Paul warned the church at Corinth about the attitudes represented by murmuring and complaining. In 1 Corinthians 10:10 he reminded them that when the children of Israel complained, fiery serpents began to destroy them. This record of Israel's sin was written so that we could learn from Israel's mistakes and not step outside of the blessings of God into the "fiery bites of serpents."

When we allow the wrong attitudes about life to overcome us, we allow ourselves to be lowered into the spiritual jurisdiction of the devil! This is, many times, how can "hit" Christians. As elementary as these things may sound, it either is amazing that many Christians are ignorant of or fail to live by these authentic governing principles of God.

9. Secret Societies – Many people are invited to be a part of different secret societies or fraternities. To join these societies or fraternities they are making a vow or oath, and in doing so, they are giving themselves over to the devil, but do not know it.

10. Works of the Flesh - When we yield to any work of the flesh such as pride, fear, strife, anger, or lust and, get involved in sin through disobedience to the instructions of God's Word and the Holy Spirit, we veer off course and lose altitude. Consider the evil work of strife as an example. When a believer gets into strife, he actually has placed in their lives. (See James 3:14-16)

Paul told Timothy in 2 Timothy 2:24-26 that those who entered into strife must, "... recover themselves out of the snare of the devil, who was taken captive by him..." Descending into satan jurisdiction will also result if one yields to demonic spirits.

When a person submits to a particular demon's influence, then that spirit gains a level of jurisdiction in their life.

When a believer walks in disobedience to God's Word and His will, they get on the devil's territory, and he has a right to attack them. Yielding to the works of the flesh or demonic influence, whether strife, lust, or anything else, gives satan jurisdiction in believers' lives.

The devil cannot launch successful attacks against us unless we yield to fleshly and demonic works like fear, doubt, strife or sin. In fact, when we stand firm, trusting God's Word, we can "pass through the fire and not be burned."

There are so many beautiful scriptures like Psalms 23:4 and Isaiah 43:1-3 that teach us if we walk with the Lord, we can pass through real storms and not even be fazed! Right in the presence of our enemies, we can have a table of God's provision spread before us!

11. Ignorance of the Word - Another way that we give place to the devil and get over onto his "turf" is through ignorance of God's Word. When we are ignorant of the Word, we are ignorant of God's will, ignorant of satan operations, and ignorant of our authority as believers. (See Hosea 4:6)

According to 2 Corinthians, 2:11 says, "Lest satan should get an advantage of us: for we are not ignorant of his devices."

satan cannot get an advantage over us when we are aware of his devices. Not being ignorant means that satan cannot gain an advantage over us. However, if we are ignorant it is possible for him to gain the upper hand.

Also, 1 Peter 5:8 reveals that if believers do not stay sober minded and aware of satan activity, then through ignorance he will take advantage of them. Ignorance of operations in the realm of the spirit is not bliss. Sometimes it can cost you your life! The Word of God is like an earth suit that protects us from the "hostile" and contaminating the environment we live in.

The Psalmist declared in Psalms 17:4, "... by the word of thy lips I have kept me from the paths of the destroyer."

In John 17:14-19, Jesus spoke this same truth concerning the ability of God's Word to protect us from the enemy while we live in his domain. (See John 17:14-19).

In Luke 4:1-13, Jesus was shot at by the devil, but because He stayed within the boundaries of God's Word He was not hit. Though satan tempted him, He responded each time by saying, "It is written."

Not only did knowledge of the Word of God protect Him from satan authority but also His relationship and fellowship with the Father remained intact. By staying within the boundaries of the written Word of God, Jesus ran satan off the mountain. Jesus also received blessings from the Lord in the form of ministry from Jesus taught in Luke 6:46-49 that when we act on the Word, living within the boundaries of what God has said, in the storms will not be able to shake our lives.

All our protection from the power of the devil and the works of his cohorts comes from abiding in the Word.

1 John 1:7 states: "But if we walk in the light, as he is in the light, we have fellowship one with another and the blood of Jesus Christ his Son cleanseth us from all sin."

When we walk in the light, that is, when we walk in the revelation of God's Word, then the blood of Jesus operates in our lives, not only as the cleansing agent but also as the protecting agent. A believer who is ignorant of what belongs to him; according to God's Word is a believer who is walking unprotected and unarmed in life's war.

12. Failing to Stand - Another way we give place to the devil merely is by failing to take a stand against him. James 4:8 states that as we resist the devil, he will flee. satan does not have a legal right to devour the believer, but because he is an outlaw, he will "break the law" and function as he wills until someone exercises authority over him. It is not only essential to have knowledge of God's Word but consciously act upon that knowledge.

It is not only important to know about satan devices and your authority over him, but you must resist him and refuse him any room to operate in your life. (See 1 Peter 5:8-9)

Many believers fail to recognize the totality of what Jesus meant in Matthew 16:19 when he said, "... I will give unto thee the keys of the kingdom of heaven." He went on to state that, "Whatsoever thou shalt bind on earth shall be bound in heaven: And whatsoever thou shalt loose on earth shall be loosed in heaven." Jesus was simply saying that what we allow God allows. What we allow the devil to do, he has the right to do by default and neglect on our part.

Jesus said in John 17 that we are in the world but are not of the world. In John 16:33 Jesus said that in the world we would have tribulation, but 1 John 5:4 teaches us that the victory that overcomes the world is our faith. Faith, which is an aggressive stand on God's Word, is necessary if we desire to quench all the fiery darts of the enemy.

13. Fear - When the believer succumbs to the force of fear, he most definitely lowers his altitude within the range of satan jurisdiction.

1 John 4:18; says that fear has torment "There is no fear in love; but perfect love casteth out fear: because fear hath torment. He that feareth is not made perfect in love."

Hebrews 2:14 and 15 teach us that it is through fear that satan holds men in bondage. "Forasmuch then as the children are partakers of flesh and blood, he also himself likewise took part of the same; that through death he might destroy him that had the power of death. That is, the devil; and deliver them who through fear of death were all their lifetime subject to bondage."

The devil dominates the lives of those who succumb to the force of fear. God's Word calls this domination bondage. Fear imprisons one's heart and releases the power of satan destruction in their life, by yielding to fear believers descend.

14. Unforgiveness - Believers place themselves well within the range of the devil's fiery darts when they choose to walk in unforgiveness and resentment. In Matthew 18:23-35, Jesus taught a parable that explains very clearly and strongly this truth.

Matthew 18:34 – 35; "And his lord was worth, and delivered him to the tormentors, till he should pay all that was due unto him. So likewise, shall my heavenly Father do also unto you, if ye from your hearts forgive not everyone his brother their trespasses."

It always troubled me that verses 34 and 35 of this passage seemed to teach that the Lord turns us over to the tormentors if we fail to forgive. It seemed to contradict to the loving nature of our Lord that he would deliver us up to the devil. Nevertheless, when I realized the truth of the law of spiritual jurisdiction, I understood what was really taking place.

When we are in blatant and conscious rebellion to a commandment as important as the law of forgiveness, then through that act of disobedience we place ourselves into the enemy's territory of operation. If you have a guest in your home that has committed a crime, when the police come and ask for him, you would have to "deliver him" to the police!

So also, if we refuse to forgive and choose, therefore, to walk in unforgiveness, when satan comes to attack us, God is obligated by spiritual law to "deliver" us to the enemy's demands. Thus, Matthew 18:23-35 is not a matter of God punishing us. God does not need the help of the devil to teach us lessons.

God has to comply with the spiritual laws He has established. Though they were established to protect us, when we break them, they result in negative consequences, and even to our own harm.

14. Disobedience to the Holy Spirit's Voice - We can readily see the importance of obeying the written dictations of God that are spoken to our hearts by the Holy Spirit.
Deuteronomy 28:15 says, "But it shall come to pass, if thou wilt not hearken unto the voice of the Lord the God, to observe to do all his commandments and his statutes which I command thee this day; that all these curses shall come upon thee and overtake thee." Notice here that we are not only instructed to observe all of God's commandments, but we are told to hearken unto His voice.

Jesus clearly and explicitly said of the Holy Spirit's ministry that He would, "...guide...speak... (And) show us things to come" (John 16:13)

Many times, Christians give a place to the devil when they fail to heed the directions of the Holy Spirit. Saints of God, hearkening unto the voice of the Holy Spirit is an essential factor in remaining outside satan range of attack. God knows what lies in the future concerning us, and by His Spirit, He will help us safely navigate around the snares of the enemy.

Summary

Again, as we examine the Holy Scriptures, according to 2 Corinthians 4:4 that satan is the god of this world system. lucifer was in the Garden of Eden in the form of the serpent. Apparently, he had already rebelled against God, becoming satan (i.e., The Adversary). His goal was to deceive Eve and ultimately Adam. Who is this person lucifer, satan, the devil, and the dragon. We have primarily three scriptures Ezekiel 28:12-13, Isaiah 14:12-15, and Revelation 12:7-9.

The devil may have the right to shoot at us while we live here on this planet, but we can walk in the place where his attacks are ineffective against us. Living outside satan range of authority by abiding in God, His Word, and in obedience to Holy Spirit are vital to living the abundant, victorious life that Jesus came to give. What does Jesus' explanation tell us concerning the characteristics and capabilities of evil spirits? They have an intellect and will; they vary in level of wickedness; they are communal; they have limited power (require rest); they can travel; they can enter and live in bodies; they communicate with other evil spirits, and they can recognize or discern the spiritual state of a person. They can attack us in various ways.

Chapter 7
List of strongman and associated spirits

A. SPIRIT OF DIVINATION
- Fortune teller/Soothsayer - Micah 5:12; Isaiah 2:6
- Warlock/Witch, Sorcerer - Exodus 22:18
- Rebellion - I Samuel 15:22
- Stargazer, Zodiac, Horoscopes - Isaiah 47:13; Leviticus 19:26; Jeremiah 10:2
- Hypnotist/Enchanter - Deuteronomy 18:11; Isaiah 19:3
- Drugs - Galatians 5:20; Revelation 9:21,18:23, 21:8,
- Water Witching - Hosea 4:12
- Magic - Exodus 7:11, 8:7; 9:11;

B. FAMILIAR SPIRIT
- Necromancer - Deuteronomy 18:11; 1 Chronicles 10:13
- Medium - 1 Samuel 28
- Clairvoyant - 1 Samuel 28:7-8
- Spiritualist - 1 Samuel 28
- Yoga - Jeremiah 29:8
- Drugs - Hallucinogens Revelation 9:21, 18:23;
- Passive Mind - Dreamers - Jeremiah 23:16, 25, 32;
- Peeping & Muttering - Isaiah 8:19, 29:4, 59:3
- False Prophecy - Isaiah 8:19, 29:4

C. SPIRIT OF JEALOUSY
- Murder - Genesis 4:8
- Anger/Rage - Genesis 4:5-6; Proverbs 6:34, 14:29, Proverbs 22:24-25, 29:22-23
- Hate - Genesis 37:3-4, 8 1 Thessalonians 4:8
- Revenge/Spite - Proverbs 6:34, 14:16-17
- Cruelty - Song of Solomon 8:6; Proverbs 27:4
- Jealousy - Numbers 5:14; Song of Solomon 8:6
- Cause Divisions - Galatians 5:19

- Extreme Competition - Genesis 4:4-5
- Contention - Proverbs 13:10
- Envy - Proverbs 14:30
- Strife - Proverbs 10:12

D. LYING SPIRIT
- Strong Deceptions - 2 Thessalonians 2:9-13
- Flattery - Psalm 78:36; Proverbs 20:19, 26:2, 29:5
- Superstitions - 1 Timothy 4:7
- Accusations - Revelation 12:10; Psalm 31:18
- False Prophecy - Jeremiah 23:16-17, 27:9-10
- Religious Bondages - Galatians 5:1
- Slander - Proverbs 10:18
- Gossip - 1 Timothy 6:20; 2 Timothy 2:16
- False Teachers - 2 Peter 2:1
- Lies - 2 Chronicles 18:22; Proverbs 6:16-19;

E. PERVERSE SPIRIT
- Wounded Spirit - Proverbs 15:14
- Evil Actions - Proverbs 17:20, 23
- Atheist - Proverbs 14:2; Romans 1:30
- Foolish - Proverbs 1:22, 19:1
- Doctrinal Error - Isaiah 19:14
- Contentions - Philippians 2:14-16; 1 Timothy 6:4-5;
- Filthy Mind - Proverbs 2:12, 23:33
- Chronic Worrier - Proverbs 19:3
- Homosexuality - Romans 1:17-32; 2 Timothy 3:2
- Incest
- Child Abuse
- Pornography
- Twisting the Word - Acts 13:10; II Peter 2:14

F. SPIRIT OF HAUGHTINESS
- Pride - Proverbs 6:16-17, 16:18-19; 28:25;
- Arrogant / Smug - 2 Sam 22:28; Jeremiah 48:29; Isa. 2:11,
- Obstinate - Proverbs 29:1; Daniel 5:20
- Idleness - Ezekiel 16:49-50
- Scornful - Proverbs 1:22; 3:34; 21:24; 29:8;
- Rebellion - 1 Samuel 15:23; Proverbs 13:10
- Contentions - Proverbs 13:10
- Strife - Proverbs 28:25
- Self-Righteousness - Luke 18:11-12
- Rejection of God - Psalm 10:4; Jeremiah 43:2
- Self-Deception - Jeremiah 49:16; Obadiah 1:3

G. SPIRIT OF HEAVINESS
- Excessive Mourning - Isaiah 6:13; Luke 4:18
- Insomnia - Nehemiah 2:2
- Self-Pity - Psalm 69:20
- Sorrow/Grief - Nehemiah 2:2; Proverbs 15:13
- Broken Hearted - Psalm 69:20; Proverbs 12:18, 15:3; 13,18:14; Luke 4:18
- Despair/Dejection/Hopelessness - 2 Corinthians 1:8-9
- Heaviness - Isaiah 61:3
- Depression - Isaiah 61:3 ▫ Suicidal Tendencies - Mark 9
- Inner Hurt/Torn Spirit - Luke 4:18; Proverbs 18:14, 26:22

H. SPIRIT OF WHOREDOMS
- Unfaithfulness/Adultery - Ezekiel 16:15, 28; Proverbs 5:1-14
- Spirit/Soul/Body Prostitution - Ezekiel 16:15, 28; Proverbs 5:1-14
- Love of Money - Proverbs 15:27; 1 Timothy 6:7-14
- Chronic Dissatisfaction - Ezekiel 16:28
- Fornication - Hosea 4:13-19
- Idolatry - Judges 2:17; Ezekiel 16; Hosea 4:12

- Excessive Appetite - 1 Corinthians 6:13-16; Philippians 3:19
- Worldliness - James 4:4

I. SPIRIT OF INFIRMITY
- Bent Body/Spine - Luke 13:11
- Impotent/Frail/Lame -John 5:5; Acts 3:2; 4:9
- Asthma/Hay Fever/Allergies - John 5:5
- Arthritis - John 5:5
- Lingering Disorders - Luke 13:11; John 5:5
- Cancer - Luke 13:11; John 5:4
- Weakness - Luke 13:11; John 5:5
- Oppression - Acts 10:38

J. DEAF AND DUMB SPIRIT
- Dumbness - Mark 9:2a
- Tearing - Mark 9:18, 20, 26
- Mental Illness - Matthew 17:15; Mark 5:5, 9:17
- Foaming at the Mouth - Luke 9:39; Mark 9:39
- Seizures/Epilepsy - Mark 9:18, 20, 26
- Suicidal - Mark 9:22
- Gnashing Teeth - Mark 9:18
- Burn - Mark 9:22
- Drown - Mark 9:22
- Pining Away - Mark 9:18
- Blindness - Matthew 12:22
- Crying - Mark 9:26
- Prostration - Mark 9:26
- Ear Problems - Mark 9:25, 26

K. SPIRIT OF BONDAGE
- Fears - Romans 8:15
- Addictions - (Drugs, Cigarettes, Alcohol, Food, etc.) Romans 8:15; II Peter 2:19
- Fear of Death - Hebrews 2:14, 15; Captivity of satan 2 Peter 2:19.
- Bondage of Sin - 2 Timothy 2:26
- Servant of Corruption - Romans 7:23; Luke 8:26-29; Acts 8:23; John 8:34; Romans 6:16
- Compulsive Sin - Proverbs 5:22

L. SPIRIT OF FEAR
- Fears/Phobias - Isaiah 13:7-8; 2 Timothy 1:7
- Torment/Horror - Psalm 55:5; I John 4:18
- Heart Attacks - Psalm 55:4 Luke 21:26; John 14:27
- Nightmares/Terrors - Psalm 91:5-6
- Fear of Death - Psalm 55:4; Hebrews 2:14, 15
- Anxiety/Stress - 1 Peter 5:7
- Untrusting/Doubt - Matthew 8:26; Revelation 21:8
- Fear of Man - Proverbs 29:25
-

M. SEDUCING SPIRITS
- Hypocritical Lies — 1 Timothy 4:1; Proverbs 1222
- Seared Conscience — 1 Timothy 4:1; James 1:14
- Deception — 2 Timothy 3:13; 1 John 2:18-26; Romans 7:11; 2 Thessalonians 2:10
- Attractions — Fascination by False Prophets,
- False Signs and Wonders — Mark 13:22
- Fascination to Evil Ways, Objects of Persons - Proverbs 12:26
- Seducers, Enticers - 1 Timothy 4:1, 2 Timothy 3:13; Proverbs 1:10
- Wander from Truth - 2 Timothy 3:13; Deut.13:6-8

N. SPIRIT OF ANTI-CHRIST
- Denies Deity of Christ - 1 John 4:3; 2 John 7
- Denies Atonement - 1 John 4:3
- Against Christ and His Teaching - 2 Thessalonians 2:4; I John 4:3
- Humanism - 2 Thessalonians 2:3, 7
- Worldly Speech and Actions - 1 John 4:5
- Teachers of Heresies - 1 John 2:18-19
- Against Christians - Revelation 13:7
- Deceiver - 2 Thessalonians 2:4; 2 John 7
- Lawlessness - 2 Thessalonians 2:3-12

O. SPIRIT OF ERROR
- Error - Proverbs 14:22, 1 John 4:6; 2 Peter 3:16, 17
- Unsubmissive - Proverbs 29:1; 1 John 4:6
- False Doctrines - 1 Timothy 6:20-21; 2 Timothy 4:3; Titus 3:10; John 4:1-6
- Unteachable - Proverbs 10:17; 12:1, 13:18, Proverbs 15:10, 12, 32
- Servant of Corruption – 2 Peter 2:19
- Contentions - James 3:16
- New Age Movement - 2 Thessalonians; 2 Peter 2:10

Chapter 8
Biblical Curses

1. The Curse causeless shall not come (Proverbs 26:2). Any sin worthy of death is also cursed by God (Deuteronomy 21:22)
2. Those who curse or mistreat Jews (Deuteronomy 27:26; Genesis 27:29, 12:3; Numbers 24:9)
3. Those who are willing deceivers; (Jos. 9:23; Jeremiah 48:10; Mal. 1:14; Gen. 27:12)
4. An adulterous woman (Numbers 5:27)
5. Disobedience to the Lord's Commandments (Deuteronomy 11:28; Daniel 9:11; Jeremiah 11:3)
6. Idolatry (Jer. 44:8; Deut. 29:19, 5:8,9; Exodus 20:5)
7. Those who keep or own cursed objects; (Deuteronomy 7:25; Joshua 6:18)
8. Those who refuse to come to the Lord's help (Judges 5:23)
9. House of the wicked (Proverbs 3:33)
10. He who gives not to the poor (Proverbs 28:27)
11. The earth by reason of man's disobedience (Isaiah 24:3-6)
12. Jerusalem is a curse to all nations if Jews rebel against God. (Jeremiah 26:6)
13. Thieves and those who swear falsely by the Lord's Name; (Zechariah 5:4)
14. Ministers who fail to give the glory to God (Malachi 3:9; Revelation 1:6)
15. Those who rob God of tithes & offerings (Malachi 3:9; Haggai 1:6-9)
16. Those who hearken unto their wives rather than God; (Genesis 3:17)

17. Those who lightly esteem their parents (Deuteronomy 27:16)
18. Those who make graven images (Deuteronomy 27:15, 5:8; Exodus 20:4)
19. Those who willfully cheat people out of their property; (Deuteronomy 27:17)
20. Those who take advantage of the blind (Deuteronomy 27:18)
21. Those who oppress strangers, widows or fatherless (Deuteronomy 27:19; Exodus 22:22-24)
22. He who lies with his father's wife (Deut. 27:20)
23. He who lies with any beast (Deuteronomy 27:21; Ex. 22:19)
24. He who lies with his sister (Deuteronomy 27:22)
25. Those who smite their neighbors secretly (Deut. 27:24)
26. Those who take money to slay the innocent (Deuteronomy 27:25)
27. Adulterers (Deut. 22:22-27, Job 24:15-18)
28. The proud (Psalm 119:21)
29. Those who trust in man and not the Lord (Jeremiah 17:5)
30. Those who do the work of the Lord deceitfully (Jer. 48:10)
31. He who keep back his sword from blood, (Jeremiah 48:10; I Kings 20:35-42)
32. Those who reward evil for good (Proverbs 17:13)
33. Illegitimate children (Deuteronomy 23:2)
34. Children born from incestuous unions (Genesis 19:36-38)
35. Murderers (Exodus 21:12)
36. To murder indirectly (Exodus 21:14).
37. Children who strike their parents (Exodus 21:15)
38. Kidnappers (Exodus 21:16; Deuteronomy 24:7)
39. Those who curse their parents (Exodus 21:17)
40. Those who cause the unborn to die (Exodus 21:22, 23)
41. Those who do not prevent death (Exodus 21:29)
42.

43. Those involved in witchcraft (Exodus 22:18)
44. Those who sacrifice to false gods (Exodus 22:20)
45. Those who attempt to turn anyone away from the Lord; (Deuteronomy 13:6-9)
46. Those who follow horoscopes (Deuteronomy 17:2-5)
47. Those who rebel against pastors (Deuteronomy 17:12)
48. False prophets (Deuteronomy 18:19-22)
    Women who do not keep their virginity until they are married (Deut. 22:13-21)
49. Parents who do not discipline their children, but honor them above God (I Samuel 2:17; 27-36)
50. Those who curse their rulers (I Kings 2:8, 9; Exodus 22:28)
51. Those who teach rebellion against the Lord; (Jeremiah 28:16, 17)
52. Those who refuse to warn them of sin (Ezekiel 3:18-21)
53. Those who defile the Sabbath (Ex. 31:14; Num. 15:32-36)
54. Those who sacrifice human beings (Leviticus 20:2)
55. Participants in séances and fortune telling (Lev 20:6)
56. Homosexual and lesbian relationships (Lev 20:13)
57. Sexual intercourse during menstruation (Lev 20:18)
58. Necromancers and fortune tellers (Lev 20:27)
59. Those who blaspheme the Lord's Name (Lev 24:15, 16)
60. Those who are carnally minded (Romans 8:6)
61. Sodomy (anal sex) (Genesis 19:13, 24, 25)
62. Rebellious children (Deuteronomy 21:18-21)

Chapter 9
Prayer a key in spiritual warfare

Introduction

Moffat's translation of Ephesians 6:18, "quoted reads, 'Praying with all manner of prayer... Another translation says, "Praying with all kinds of prayer..." In today's lesson, we will look at some of the different kinds of prayer in the New Testament.

Just as there are numerous different games, which come under the general, classification of sports, so there are many different kinds of prayer that we often lump together under one general category of prayer. We need to realize that as certain rules govern certain games in the area of sports, so there are certain principles or rules, spiritual laws so to speak, that govern certain kinds of praying.

The ones that might apply to one type of prayer would not necessarily apply to another type of prayer. In sports, the rules, which apply to baseball, would not apply to football. If one tried to use the same rules for both games, he would get terribly confused.

Multiplied Prayer Power

Deuteronomy 32:30 (NKJV) "*How could one chase a thousand, And two put ten thousand to flight, unless their Rock had sold them, and the LORD had surrendered them?*"

We may be mighty in prayer alone, but we can be mightier with someone joining us. We read in the above verse that one can chase a thousand, but two can put ten thousand to flight.

With someone agreeing with us in prayer, we can do ten times as much as we can do by ourselves. There does not have to be a significant number. Just a husband and wife will do. Just two, three = twenty thousand, four=thirty thousand.

Spirit of Prayer

Dr. Gary L. Wood, in from book a Place called Heaven "While I was with Jesus, He showed me the earth. It was as if I was looking at the pictures the astronauts send to us on earth from the satellite; only three rings encircled the earth. Inside the first ring was the earth's atmosphere, I saw hundreds of evil spirits. This is the devil's domain. The evil spirits would target people and try to deceive them. If people accept the lies as truth, many more demons will swarm in like flies.

They would then begin to fall into the temptations of them, and their lives would begin to fall apart. The demons have the power to make people tell lies, cheat, steal, commit adultery, and speak evil against one another. It was like the people become puppets on a string.

Then Jesus showed me that when a child of God got down on their knees before Him, praying in the name of Jesus, with faith, their prayers would shoot out into the heavens like barbed arrows. An army of angelic forces would appear, prepared for a battle to destroy the demons' effectiveness. The more prayers of faith, there were the demons would retreat. However, if doubt and unbelief were spoken, the demons would begin to overcome.

The Lord told me that as time grows closer to his return, demon activity would become more rampant. The devil knows that the final curtain is being drawn, and his time is running out. Millions of demons and their evil power abound all around us. Why are we so besieged by demonic powers? It is because we pray so little. The results are immoral, perversion, child abuse, poverty, abortion, wars, revolutions, pornography, the occults, an increase in crime, and sicknesses such as AIDS, just to name a few.

> **Ephesians 6:13-18;** *13 Wherefore take unto you the whole armour of God, that ye may be able to withstand in the evil day, and having done all, to stand. 14 Stand therefore, having your loins girt about with truth, and having on the breastplate of righteousness; 15 And your feet shod with the preparation of the gospel of peace; 16 Above all, taking the shield of faith, wherewith ye shall be able to quench all the fiery darts of the wicked. 17 And take the helmet of salvation, and the sword of the Spirit, which is the word of God: 18 Praying always with all prayer and supplication in the Spirit, and watching thereunto with all perseverance and supplication for all saints;*

Put on your armor and take a stand against the workings of the devil. You can only arm yourself with the Word of God. If you do not read or study the Bible, you have no defense against the forces of darkness that are always at work to defeat you. With faith, tear down the strongholds of the devil and surrender your life to the Holy Spirit.

I have come to believe that, beyond any doubt, the greatest need of mankind is prayer. Our only hope to destroy the demonic powers in the world today is through the *Spirit of Prayer.*"

(A.) Prayer of Thanksgiving, Praise, Worship (Acts 13:1-4, Acts 16:25, 1 Thessalonians 523)

The Prayer of Worship
Acts 13:1-4

Not only do we need our individual private prayer life, but we also need the different kinds of prayer. We read of a group in the New Testament church who had such a service.

> *Acts 13:1-4;* "*¹Now there were in the church that was at Antioch certain prophets and teachers; as Barnabas, and Simeon that was called Niger, and Lucius of Cyrene, and Manaen, which had been brought up with Herod the tetrarch, and Saul. ²As they ministered to the Lord, and fasted, the Holy Ghost said, separate me Barnabas and Saul for the work whereunto I have called them. ³And when they had fasted and prayed, and laid their hands on them, they sent them away. ⁴So they, being sent forth by the Holy Ghost, departed unto Selcucia; and from thence, they sailed to Cyprus.*

Today when Christians gather for a church service, we mostly minister to one another. Our services are designed that way. We sing songs, but in very few of them do we minister to the Lord; we minister to one another. We sing special solo numbers, but still, we are not ministering to the Lord; we are ministering to one another. When we pray in church, our praying is primarily a petition. We are petitioning the Lord to move in our midst, to manifest Himself among us, and to meet our individual needs. Then when the minister stands to speak, he is not ministering to the Lord; he is ministering to the congregation.

When the service is over, if we do have a time of waiting on God in prayer, this usually consists of petitioning prayer again. We come not necessarily to minister to the Lord but to pray and seek God on our own behalf.

However, the Christians we read about in the account above in Acts 13:1-4 came together and "ministered to the Lord, and fasted..." (Verse 2), More than one person was involved in this account, for it says, "As they ministered to the Lord, and fasted..." This is the true prayer of worship.

1. God's Desire for Man's Praise

God made man so He would have someone with whom to have fellowship. He made man for His own pleasure. It is true that God is concerned about us and wants to meet our every need. God needs even more than that He wants our love, our worship, and fellowship with Him. He is our Father for we are born of God No earthly parent ever enjoyed the fellowship of his children more than God enjoys the fellowship of His sons and daughters.

2. The Power of Praise

Let me call your attention to the fact that this is the kind of atmosphere in God has told me He has blotted out my transgressions and then does not remember what they were in Isaiah 43:22;

"As they ministered to the Lord, and fasted, the Holy Ghost said... With hearts yielded to the Lord, full of love and praise, the Holy Spirit can manifest Himself and make known God's will and leading for the lives of His children. (Acts 13:1)

3. The story illustrates the Power of praise

A minister told me of an experience he had once, which illustrates the power of praise. Once very early in his ministry, while he was a young evangelist, he was staying at the pastor's home during one of his revival meetings. During the night, a call came to the pastor to come to pray for a baby who was having convulsions.

Relating the experience to me, he said, "We rebuked the devil, we prayed at the top of our voices and went through all the motions that we sometimes feel are necessary to get God to hear our prayers. After about forty minutes of such rigorous praying, the child was no better but continued having convulsions."

I had done about all I knew to do. I had done everything I had seen anybody else do. However, nothing happened. Then, as I got quiet, it seemed that the group who were gathered there to pray also grew quiet. Then the pastor's wife began to say softly, 'Praise the Lord, praise the Lord,' and praises began rolling from her lips. She continued in this spirit of praise for about ten minutes. Finally, one by one all of us picked it up until we were all praising God. In the midst of that, atmosphere the child's convulsions ceased, and he fell asleep.

"We stood around for a while rejoicing in the Lord. Then, while we were taking the child awakened and went back into convulsions. We became alarmed and started to pray and rebuke the devil. We anointed the child with oil and laid hands on him. We went through all the usual maneuvers again, but nothing seemed to help."

"Then when we settled down again, the pastor's wife began to praise the Lord, ministering to the Lord and telling Him how much she loved Him. We all joined in, and shortly the child's convulsions stopped, and he went to sleep, permanently healed. That night I witnessed the power of praise."

The prayer of worship worked when nothing else did in this instance. As these Christians, like those in the Early Church, "ministered to the Lord," the Holy Ghost moved and made manifest the mighty power of God.

In the sixteenth chapter of Acts, we have the story of Paul and Silas in Philippi We read of their arrest, how they were beaten with many stripes and cast into prison.

> **Acts 16:22-25**; *"And the multitude rose up together against them: and the magistrates rent off their clothes, and commanded them to bear them. 23And when they had laid many stripes upon them, they cast them into prison, charging the jailer to keep them safely. 24Who, having received such a charge. Thrust them into the inner prison, and made their feet fast in the stocks. 25And at midnight. Paul and Silas prayed, and sang praises unto God: and the prisoners heard them.*

A Song at Midnight

I want to call particular attention to verse 25... Paul and Silas prayed and sang praises unto God. _" What did they have to be so happy about that they felt like singing? Surely, nothing was going right for them.

They had been our preaching the good news of the gospel and what did they get for id they were brought before the rulers, were charged and beaten, and they were cast into prison with their feet placed in stocks.

Their backs were sore and bleeding. Every part of their bodies ached. However, did they sit there moaning and complaining, crying, "Why did this have to happen to me?" No. The Bible says they "sang praises unto God."

If they had been like some of us today the scripture might have read, "And at midnight Paul and Silas griped and complained, whined and whimpered, wondering why God has allowed this to come upon them." Their conversation might have followed this line: "Paul, you still there," "Sure, we are still here. Where else could we be," "I tell you, my poor back is really hurting me. I just do not understand why God ever sent this on us. He knows that I have tried to serve Him and have done my best." That kind of attitude would have just gotten them further into trouble instead of out of it.

We can learn something here from Paul and Silas. After all, they were in trouble. They were in pain. They were in jail. Overall, it was a dark picture. One could hardly blame them for being discouraged. However, as someone has said, Paul and Silas got in jail, but they did not let the jail get in them.

This is the reason many people are defeated. Trouble comes to everyone, but our attitude toward it is what makes the difference between victory and defeat. How we look at the situation makes the difference in how we come out or whether we get out at all. In the example of Paul and Silas, we can find help for our midnight hour, for our time of testing, in an hour when the storms of life threaten to sweep us overboard.

Paul and Silas were not in Philippi on vacation. They were there to do the Lord's work. They were not out of the will of God. The first thing that some people think when adversity strikes are that they must surely be out of the Lord's will or such a thing would not have happened.

They were right in the middle of God's will. If we were to measure whether we are in God's will by whether everything runs smoothly with no hard places and no sacrifices, then Paul never did get in the will of God in his entire ministry.

He missed it from beginning to end. Let us notice something else in verse 25. "And at midnight Paul and Silas prayed, and sang praises unto God: and the prisoners heard them." They were not quiet about it. They were praising God out loud right there in jail. Not only did the prisoners hear them, but also God heard them! "And suddenly there was a great earthquake so that the foundations of the prison were shaken: and immediately all the doors were opened, and every one's bands were loosed" (Verse 26).

A Song in Battle

Let us look at the Old Testament counterpart to this story. During the reign of King Jehoshaphat, the Ammonites and Moabites came against the Israelites. Jehoshaphat cried out to the Lord in prayer and He answered him.

2 Chronicles 20:15. 17-19, 21-22;

> *"And he said, Hearken ye, all Judah, and ye inhabitants of Jerusalem, and thou king Jehoshaphat, Thus saith the Lord unto you, Be not afraid nor dismayed by reason of this great multitude; for the battle is not yours, but God's. 17 Ye shall not need to fight in this battle; set yourselves, stand ye still, and see the salvation of the Lord with you, 0 Judah and Jerusalem: fear not, nor be dismayed; tomorrow go out against them: for the Lord will be with you. 18 And Jehoshaphat bowed his head with his face to the ground: and all Judah and the inhabitants of Jerusalem fell before the Lord, worshipping the Lord. 19 And the Levites, of the children of the Kohathites, and of the children of the Korhites, stood up to praise the Lord God of Israel with a loud voice on high. 21 And when he had consulted with the people, he appointed singers unto the Lord, and that should praise the beauty of holiness, as they went out before the army, and to say, Praise the Lord; for his mercy endureth forever. 22 And when they began to sing and to praise, the Lord set ambushments against the children of Ammon, Moab, and mount Stir, which were come against Judah; and they were smitten.*

Jehoshaphat knew that his army was no match for those of the countries banded against him. However, he knew his God was more than a match for them. He called a prayer meeting and they fasted and prayed.

The Spirit of God moved upon a young man in the congregation and he stood and prophesied. The Lord told them not to fear, for the battle was the Lord's.

The next morning when they went out against the enemy's mighty armies, they did not go against them with swords and spears but with songs of praise (Verse 21). They marched along and chanted, "Praise the Lord; for his mercy endureth forever." They sang and praised the Lord just as Paul and Silas did in jail. In their hour of trial, instead of cowering in fear the children of Israel sang praises to God just as Paul and Silas did. What was the outcome of this battle? Look at verse 22. "And when they began to sing and to praise, the Lord sent ambushments against the children of Ammon, Moab, and mount Seir, which were come against Judah; and they were smitten." When they began to sing praises unto God, He did something. They witnessed a manifestation of God's power.

Praise, a Characteristic of the Early Church,
A spirit of praise and rejoicing was a characteristic of the early church.

Luke 24:50-53;

> "And he led them out 25 far as to Bethany, and he lifted up his hands, and blessed them. [51] And it came to pass, while he blessed them, he was parted from them, and carried up into heaven. [52] And they worshipped him, and returned to Jerusalem with great joy: [53] And were continually in the temple, praising and blessing God.

After the disciples watched Jesus return to heaven, they went back to Jerusalem with hearts filled with praise and thanksgiving to God.

Then we read about them in Acts 2:46-47.

"And they, continuing daily with one accord in the temple, and breaking bread from house to house, did eat their meat with gladness and singleness of heart, Praising God, and having favor with all the people. And the Lord added to the church daily such as should be saved."

Notice the expression, "They, continuing daily with one accord... eat their meat with gladness... praising God..." With these early Christians, this was not only a spasmodic occurrence. It was not just something that happened once in a great while. The Bible uses the words "continually" and "daily."

Too many times, some Christians today will be prayed through about once every six months and will have a time of praising and blessing God. If we were writing about them, we would have to use the words "occasionally" or perhaps even "semiannually." However, of the early Christians, the Bible records that they "were continually in the temple, praising and blessing God."

1 Thessalonians 5:23;

And the very God of peace sanctify you wholly; and I pray God your whole spirit and soul and body be preserved blameless unto the coming of our Lord Jesus Christ.

If we want to see the same manifestations of power that the early church had, we are going to have to see the same manifestations of praise that they had.

(B.) Prayer of Petition \ Faith

(Matthew 21:21-22, Mark 11:24, 1 John 5:14-15)

"The prayer of petition must be a prayer of faith. This is primarily an individual situation. It concerns your desires. It concerns your needs and problems. It is your praying, not someone else praying with you or for you. It is not someone else agreeing with you in prayer. When you pray, you believe that you receive, and if you will do that, you will have it. He is concerned about our needs and wants to meet them for us. This is primarily the prayer that most individual Christian pray.

In the Old Testament God promised His people more than just spiritual blessings. He promised them that they would prosper financially and materially. He told them that He would take sickness away from their midst and would give them long life.

> **Exodus 23:26;**"*The number of thy days I will fulfill*".

He told them that if they kept His commandments, they would eat the good of the land. God is just as interested in His people today as He was then. He is concerned about everything that touches our lives; He has made provision for us.

3 John 1:2; "*Beloved, I wish above all things that thou mayest prosper and be in health, Even as thy soul prosperth*"

Jesus said. "If ye then, being evil, know how to give good gifts unto your children, how much more shall your Father which is in heaven give good things to them that ask him?"

(Matthew 7:11). We must realize that it is God's will that our needs: spiritual, physical and material needs be met.

Jesus is at the right hand of the Father, the place of authority, and we are seated with Him, we have died with Him and have been raised with Him. According to Ephesians 1:20; 2:5, 6;

Some people think that they should conclude every prayer with the words, "If it be thy will." They claim Jesus prayed this way. However, Jesus prayed this way on only one occasion. When He stood at Lazarus' tomb, He did not say, "... if it be thy will ..."

He said, "I thank you because you hear me always," then He commanded Lazarus to come forth. This prayer was to change something. Anytime we are praying to do something or change something, and we need not put an "if" in our prayer. If we do, we are using the wrong rule, and it will not work, we need to claim God's promise for our petition and "believe that ye receive them." (1 John 5:14-15)

C.) Prayer of Binding and Loosing

(Matthew 18:18-20, Deuteronomy 32:30)

Of all the many prayer promises in the Bible, perhaps none is more significant than the one in Matthew 18:19, the memory teat quoted below. Yet many dedicated Christians go through life knowing the Word, having read and even studied this promise, without really appropriating it in their own lives. God did not put all of these promises relative to prayer in the Bible just to fill up space. They are there for our benefit. They are there for us to use.

In order, Roger the full impact of what Jesus is saying in this verse of scripture; let us look at the verse preceding and following it.

> **Matthew 18:18-20**"*Verily I say unto you, whatsoever ye shall bind on earth shall be bound in heaven: and whatsoever ye shall loose on earth shall be loosed in heaven. 19 Again I say unto you, that if two of you shall agree on earth as touching anything that they shall ask, it shall be done for them of my Father, which is in heaven. 20 For where two or three are gathered together in my name, there am I in the midst of them.*"

Notice the phrase in verse 19, "it shall be done for them of my Father which is in heaven." The strongest assertion, one can make in the English language is to say "I shall" or "I will." We cannot make a stronger statement than that. In this scripture, Jesus promised, 'It shall be done for them of my Father which is in heaven."

He also said, "*If ye shall ask any thing in my name, I will do it*" (John 14:14)

1. Authority to Bind and Loosen

Looking at verse 20 of the above passage, "For where two or three are gathered together in my name, there am I in the midst of them," we usually apply this to a church service. Of course, it can refer to this, but what Jesus was really saying here is that wherever these two people are who agree, He is right there to make it good. Jesus was bringing out the fact that whatever we bind on earth shall be bound in heaven, and whatever we lose on earth shall be loosed in heaven. Heaven will back us up in what we do on earth. We have the authority to lose and to bind.

Instead of using this authority, however, too many folks just let the devil bind them. They think they cannot help it if they are defeated and depressed. They think there nothing they can do about it, but they can do something about it by acting upon this scripture by agreeing in prayer with just one other believer.

2. Story illustration

Dr. Kenneth E. Hagin shares during 1957 our nation experienced economic recession. Oregon was a state, which felt the recession quite desperate. At the time, a preacher was preaching a revival campaign in Salem, Oregon. As he reached on the subject of the agreement prayer, a couple in the church decided to claim this promise and make work for them. They had a lot, which they had been trying to sell for two years with no success.

Now that times were so difficult, it seemed impossible able to sell it at all. Yet, they agreed in prayer that with the Lord's help they would be able to sell it. When the man visited a real estate agent, he was told that since the agent had not been able to sell the lot for a lot when times were good, there was little hope that it would sell now. He did suggest that the man talk to a client who had previously been interested in the lot. The agent was not too optimistic, however, said that if this client did not buy the lot, to come back and he would list it again and try once more to sell it.

Remembering Jesus' promise concerning agreement in prayer, the man approached the client with an offer to see the lot again (at the same price they had discussed before).

This time the man said he would take it. For two years, this couple had been in financial trouble, desperately needing to sell their lot. They could have had the money all the time if only they exercised their authority by agreeing in prayer "it shall be done for them of my Father which is in heaven." Instead of believing with the heart and saying it with the mouth, they had been praying that God would do something about it.

They realized now that they should have done something about it. We have our part to play. When we make our move, then God moves.

(D.) Prayer of Intercession

Genesis 18:23-36; Isaiah 64:7; Ezekiel 22:30; Romans 8:26, 27

Question #1. What is the prayer of intercession? The word "intercede" means to act between two parties with the thought of reconciling the two of them.

Therefore, the prayer of intercession is standing in the gap in prayer on behalf of another. Typically, we intercede for the unsaved. God said something to Israel through the prophet Isaiah that shows that God desires His people to intercede on behalf of others.

Isaiah 64:7 (NKJV)"*And there is no one who calls on Your name, Who stirs himself up to take hold of You; For You have hidden Your face from us, And have consumed us because of our iniquities.*"

This verse implies that if someone had stirred himself up to pray and intercedes in answer to the call upon God, judgment on the nation of Isaiah could have been stayed or stopped! Let us look at a similar statement by Ezekiel.

Question #2. Isaiah 64:7 emphasizes that the judgment on the nation of Israel have been stopped. How?

Ezekiel 22:30 (NKJV) *"So I sought for a man among them who would make a wall, and stand in the gap before Me on behalf of the land, that I should not destroy it; but I found no one."*

Do you realize what these verses are saying? God looks for people of prayer to stand in the gap, to make up the hedge, and to intercede so that people's lives can be spared.

Abraham's Intercession

In Genesis chapter 18, we see the example of Abraham as one who stood in the gap on behalf of others. When Abraham became aware of the impending judgment upon the inhabitants of Sodom and Gomorrah, he interceded for them. Let us look at the example of Abraham in Genesis chapter 18, who interceded or stood in the gap for others. (Genesis 18:23-32).

When Abraham asked the Lord to spare the city if He should find fifty righteous people, the Lord said, "... If I find in Sodom fifty righteous within the city, then I will spare all the people for their sakes" (Genesis 18:26)

Then Abraham said, "*Lord, I'd just like to speak a little further to you, if you don't mind. (I am putting this in my own words, but this is the essence of what Abraham said) If there are forty-five righteous people there, would you spare the place for forty-five?*" (Genesis 18:28).

In effect, the Lord answered Abraham, "Yes, I will do it - just because you asked Me. For forty-five righteous, I will spare the thousands who are there"(Genesis 18:26)

Then Abraham continued to ask the Lord to spare Sodom and Gomorrah, even if there were only forty-five, thirty-five, thirty, or twenty righteous inhabitants. Finally, Abraham continued to ask to spare Sodom and Gomorrah for the sake of ten righteous people, and God agreed to stay judgment if ten righteous were found. Abraham surely, though there would be at least ten righteous in Sodom and Gomorrah.

Think about that! God would have spared that city which was full of corruption and immorality for the sake of ten righteous people. The Bible says God never changes - He is forever the same (Malachi 3:6) Will He not do in our day what He did in Abraham's day.

If the Old Covenant, Abraham interceded for other people and God heard him, how much more would God hear our prayers under the New Covenant?

Will He not hear our prayers for cities and nations for the sake of His children who live in them? He will if we will intercede as Abraham did! We are covenant children, just as Abraham was. However, we have an even better Covenant established upon better promises (Hebrew 8:6).

We have the authority in the Name of Jesus to help others through prayer and intercession and to effect a change in nations to the glory of God.

The Holy Spirit Helps Us Intercede

Now will see how the Holy Spirit will help us as we intercede for others. We can intercede with our understanding, as Abraham did, or we can intercede with our spirits praying in tongues or groanings and travail.
We must keep in mind that intercession can only be accomplished by the leading and guiding of the Holy Spirit.

Let us look at Romans chapter 8 to gain insight on the Holy Spirit's role as we intercede for others.

Romans 8:26 (NKJV), *"Likewise the Spirit also helps in our weaknesses. For we do not know what we should pray for as we ought, but the Spirit Himself makes intercession for us with groanings which cannot be uttered."*

1 Corinthians 14:14 (NKJV) *"For if I pray in a tongue, my spirit prays, but my understanding is unfruitful."*

Can we see the connection between Romans 8:26 and 1 Corinthians 14:14? In both of these verses, the Holy Spirit enables our spirit to pray apart from our understanding.

Question #3. How is intercession accomplished?

According to Romans 8:26, we do not always know for what to pray as we ought; we think that we to do sometimes, but we do not; We cannot possibly know in our natural mind everything we should pray about in every situation and circumstance.

Therefore, praying with our understanding sometimes falls far short of what we ought to do in praying. We should pray as much as we know in our understanding, of course. Sometimes we pray a few words in general for others salve (soothe) a person's conscience.

Ephesians 1:3, *"Blessed be the God and Father of our Lord Jesus Christ, who hath blessed us with all spiritual blessings in heavenly places in Christ:"*

You can say what you want or desire and even quote scriptures, but when it comes to prayer, many times, especially in praying for others, we do not know what to pray for, as we ought. Thank God, the Spirit helps our infirmities. An infirmity is any weakness, which would include a lack of knowledge about how to pray.

He makes intercession for us with groaning which cannot be uttered in articulate speech (Romans 8:26). This scripture does not mean prayer is something the Holy Spirit does apart from you. That would make the Holy Spirit responsible for your prayer life, and He is not. You are responsible for your own prayer life.

Notice also the Bible says in Romans 8:26 that the Holy Spirit helps the believer in prayer. The Holy Spirit is not sent to do your praying for you. He is sent to help you in every aspect of life and to help you in your life as well.

Question #4. When praying for others, what role does the Holy Spirit do and what is our responsibility?

The Holy Spirit helps the believer to pray. He helps us to intercede for others. However, the Holy Spirit does not do the praying apart from the believer.

It is our responsibility to take the time to pray and intercede for others and to obey the gentle urgings of the Holy Spirit to do so. As we yield to the Holy Spirit, we may pray in groanings according to the will of God.

Question #5. What is groaning in the Spirit?

We can also pray in other tongues at will; we do not need to wait for the Holy Spirit to prompt us. As we yield to the Holy Spirit, He will give us utterance according to the will of God. That utterance in groanings or it may be in intercession in tongues, or it may be intercession in our understanding in our native language.

Chapter 10
The Authority and Weapons of our warfare
Mark 16:17-18

God hears and answers prayer. We might as well settle that. It works. Many times, people make a stab in the dark at praying. They call it praying and let it go at that. They hope that something works out some way or somehow. We need to take our stand on God's Word and let heaven; hell, and earth know that God's Word is true and that we believe it.

We need to be able to grow in prayer. Many times, God condescends to meet us on an elementary level, but it is better when we can grow spiritually and meet Him on His level. The Bible teaches that there is a similarity between physical growth and spiritual growth. "Like newborn babies, desire the sincere milk of the word, which ye may grow thereby" (1 Peter 2:2). No one is born a fully-grown adult. We are born as babies, and we are to grow up. No one is born a full-grown Christian. Christians are newborn babies and then grow up. As we mature in the Word, we should be able to improve our prayer life.

When I was a child I prayed, "Now I lay me down to sleep..." but I do not pray that way anymore. I have grown beyond that. When we were spiritual babes, we might have prayed specific ways, but God wants us to grow spiritually. God will require more of us now than He did even a few years ago. When the light comes, and teaching is given, God requires us to walk in the light of it.

The Word of God!

We need to know the word, speak the word, confess the word, use the word. Jesus did that. Every time the devil came at Jesus, He responded with "It is written…" The Prayer of Petition revolves around praying the Word of God. When you pray the Word of God, then you are praying in agreement with God's will. ***Hebrews 4:12***

Our weapons are not only defensive in nature. Ephesians 6:17 says we have the "sword of the Spirit" which is the word of God. We do not use swords for blocking an attack. We fight offensively with a sword. We need to become comfortable with hand-to-hand combat with the enemy.

The sword of the Spirit, which is "the Word of God praying or speaking." That is all one thought. I do not know if you knew this before, but the Word of God can pray. However, it needs a vehicle, a voice, someone to speak. In other words, God needs us to pray His Word. Not only that, but the best part is that God promised us in Isaiah 55:11 that the Word of God will not return to Him void. That promise guarantees results! (*See 2 Corinthians 4:6*)

The Blood of Jesus!

The shedding of His blood on the cross was used to defeat the devil. Learn how to apply the blood of Jesus against the devil and all his demons, because "The blood of Jesus has defeated the devil, demons and the kingdom of darkness." Colossians 2:13-15.

Using the blood in spiritual warfare: *We overcome the devil when we claim (pray, sing, or state) what the blood does for us. Specifically, the blood:*

1. Redeems and cleanses me from past, present and future sins (Ephesians 1:7, 1 John 1:7)
2. Justifies me, making me righteous, as if I had never sinned (Romans 5:9, Hebrews 13:12)
3. Cleanses my mind and conscience from sin and the memories it created (Hebrews 9:14)
4. Reconciles me with God, because Jesus bore all the punishment for my sin (Romans 5:1, 1 Peter 2:24); I am forgiven for all my sins (1 John 1:9)!
5. Enables me to boldly approach God's throne without fear of punishment (Hebrews 10:19)

Daily Prayer for applying the Blood of Jesus:

The following prayer is a good one to pray before starting your day, during noontime, and before going the bed or anytime that you are going into a spiritual warfare situation.

Applying the blood of Christ should be done with understanding, reverence, and recognition of its meaning. As with all spiritual weapons, our understanding combined with belief (faith) will unleash God's power in the situation we are facing.

"Lord Jesus, I cover myself and everyone around me with the blood of Jesus. I cover all of the members of my family (State them by name) with the blood of Jesus, I cover my home, my land, my car, my finances, my marriage, my ministries, with the blood of Jesus.

In the Name of Jesus Christ, by the power of His blood, I break off every power of the Kingdom of darkness, cancel every argument in heaven that has established itself against the plans of God in my life, and spoil every attack of the enemy.

Heavenly Father, I call forth, in the name of Jesus, all of your plans and purposes for my life, and my family. As for my house, and me we shall serve the Lord. The blood of Jesus is against you devil, and you have no authority over my life, and no place in my life, In Jesus Name.

C. The name of Jesus!

This is one reason that we have many sermons with the name of Jesus. The name of Jesus has miraculous power. It is the name above every other name. It is above cancer, diabetes, depression, and every evil dictator in the Earth. Jesus has granted us access to His name. We are to go forward using the name that has the highest authority in the universe. *Philippians 2:9*

1. Believers' Rights in the Name of Jesus

> Mark 16:17-18;
>
> "*17 And these signs shall follow them that believe; In my name shall they cast out devils; they shall speak with new tongues; 18 They shall take up serpents; and if they drink any deadly thing, it shall not hurt them; they shall lay hands on the sick, and they shall recover.*"

In John 16:23-24, concerns the fact that prayer should be addressed to the Father in Jesus' name. We saw that this is the key to seeing our prayers answered.

Jesus gave us the power of attorney, or the right to use His name, not only in praying for our individual needs, but also in dealing with the devil. He said, "In my name shall they cast out devils.

When Jesus appointed the seventy disciples and sent them forth,

Luke 10:17; *"The seventy returned again with joy, saying, Lord, even the devils are subject unto us through thy name"*

In Acts 16:16-18 we read where Paul cast an evil spirit out of a girl. "But Paul, being grieved, turned and said to the spirit, I command thee in the name of Jesus Christ to come out of her. Moreover, he came out the same hour."

Jesus also said in the seventeenth verse of the above passage, "In my name. They shall speak with new tongues." Every believer has the right and can speak in tongues.

The next verse says that in Jesus name "they shall take up serpents; and if they drink any deadly thing, it shall not hurt them." This does not mean; of course, that we are to take up serpents and handle them just to try to prove something. It means that if we are accidentally bitten, as Paul was on the island of Malta, we can shake off the serpent and claim immunity in the name of Jesus.

We read in Acts 28:3-6 of how when Paul was shipwrecked and picked up some sticks to build a fire, a viper came out and fastened on his hand. The people who saw this expected him to fall dead at any moment. When he did not die, become sick, or his hand did not even become swollen, the people knew they had witnessed a miracle.

The scripture further says, "And if they drink any deadly thing, it shall not hurt them." Again, this does not mean that we can drink something poisonous just to try to prove a point. It means that if we do accidentally, we can claim immunity in the name of the Lord Jesus Christ.

Let me point out that Jesus said, "In my name... It is in His name that we can cast out devils. It is in His name that we can speak with new tongues. It is in His name that we can claim immunity if we accidentally take up serpents or drink any deadly thing. It is in His name that we can lay hands on the sick, and they shall recover. His name gives us authority to claim these things.

Notice also He said that are to lay hands on the sick. We do the laying on of hands, not Jesus. The name of Jesus belongs to me as much as my hands and feet belong to me. When awakening in the morning, I do not pray for God to give me faith to get up and walk. I get up and walk because I know my feet are there, and they are mine. Indeed, the name of Jesus is just as much mine as my hands and feet are mines, and I can use His name.

2. Power of the Spirit of Prayer

In his Place called Heaven by Dr. Gary L. Wood, "While I was with Jesus, He showed me the earth. It was as if I was looking at the pictures the astronauts send to us on earth from the satellite; only three rings encircled the earth.

Inside the first ring was the earth's atmosphere, I saw hundreds of evil spirits. The devil's domain. The evil spirits would target people and try to deceive them.

If people accept the lies as truth, many more demons will swarm in like flies. They would then begin to fall into the temptations of them, and their lives would begin to fall apart. The demons have the power to make people tell lies, cheat, steal, commit adultery, and speak evil against one another. It was like the people become puppets on a string.

Then Jesus showed me that when a child of God got down on their knees before Him, praying in the name of Jesus, with faith, their prayers would shoot out into the heavens like barbed arrows. An army of angelic forces would appear, prepared for the battle to destroy the demons' effectiveness. The more prayers of faith, there were the demons would retreat. However, if doubt and unbelief were spoken, the demons would begin to overcome.

The Lord told me that as time grows closer to his return, demon activity would become more rampant. The devil knows that the final curtain is being drawn, and his time is running out. Millions of demons and their evil power abound all around us. Why do demonic powers so besiege us? It is because we pray so little. The results are immoral, perversion, child abuse, poverty, abortion, wars, revolutions, pornography, the occults, an increase in crime, and sicknesses such as AIDS, to name a few.

A. Daily Confession of Protection Psalm 91 personalize

1. I dwelleth in the secret place of the Most High; I abide under the shadow of the Almighty.
2. I say of the LORD, *He is* my refuge and my fortress: my God; in him will I trust.
3. I am delivered from the snare of the fowler, *and* from the noisome pestilence.
4. I am covered with his feathers, and under his wings, I trust: His truth *is my* shield and buckler.
5. I am not be afraid of the terror by night; *nor* for the arrow *that* flieth by day;
6. *Nor* for the pestilence *that* walketh in darkness; *nor* for the destruction *that* wasteth at noonday.
7. A thousand shall fall at my side, and ten thousand at my right hand; *but* it shall not come near me.
8. Only with my eyes, will I behold and see the reward of the wicked.
9. Because I have made the LORD, *which is* my refuge, *even* the Most High, my habitation;
10. No evil shall befall me; neither shall any plague come nigh my dwelling.
11. For he has given his angels charge over me, to keep me in all thy ways.
12. Angels bear me up in *their* hands, lest I dash my foot against a stone.
13. I tread upon the lion and adder: the young lion and the dragon I trample under feet.
14. Because I have set my love upon HIM, He will deliver me: He will set me on high, because I have known my names (See page 115, 117, and 119).
15. I call upon HIM, and He will answer me: He *will be* with me in time of trouble; He will deliver me and honor me.
16. With long life will He will satisfy me, and show me His salvation."

D) The Armor of God

"Wherefore take unto you the whole armor of God that ye may be able to withstand in the evil day, and having done all, to stand" Ephesians 6:13.

Spiritually Dressed for Success

"Put on the whole armor of God that you may be able to stand against the wiles of the devil. For we do not wrestle against flesh and blood, but against principalities, against powers, against the rulers of the darkness of this age, against spiritual hosts of wickedness in the heavenly places;" Ephesians 6:11-12;

Belt of Truth, verse 14
- Make no compromises with the truth.
- Speak words of life.
- Move with authority.

Breastplate of Righteousness, verse 14
- Live free of condemnation.
- Approach the enemy under the covering of the blood of Jesus.
- Move with confidence.

Shoes of Peace, verse 15
- Live in unity with the Holy Spirit and people.
- Commit to God's ways and purposes.
- Confidently take what the enemy has stolen.
- Proclaim the good news to all!

Shield of Faith, verse 16
- Simply trust in God.
- Consume all the fiery arrows of the enemy.
- To train ourselves with the Word of God.

Helmet of Salvation, verse 17
- Have received salvation, which includes eternal life, deliverance, and healing through the blood of Jesus.
- Guard our minds from lies and confusion.
- Have our consciences cleansed by the blood of Jesus.

Sword of the Spirit, verse 18
- Have the Word of God in our hearts.
- Meet every attack of the enemy with the God's Word.
- Use the Word of God to cleanse us from the wounds inflicted by the enemy.

Put on your armor and take a stand against the workings of the devil. You can only arm yourself with the Word of God. If you do not read or study the Bible, you have no defense against the forces of darkness that are always at work to defeat you. With faith, tear down the strongholds of the devil and surrender your life to the Holy Spirit.

I have come to believe that, beyond any doubt, the greatest need of mankind is prayer. Our only hope to destroy the demonic powers in the world today is through the *Spirit of Prayer.*"

That you and I have access when we pray to three major weapons: In the name of Jesus, the Word of God, and the Holy Spirit. These weapons are not carnal, but spiritually strong enough to pull down strongholds and change what seems to be impossible into possible. Are you facing an impossible situation today?

1) The Power of Praise and Worship – the moment starts when an attack, begin to praise and worship God. The devil and his cohorts will run like a scared dog.

Again, this is the reason many people are defeated. Trouble comes to everyone, but our attitude toward it is what makes the difference between victory and defeat. How we look at the situation makes the difference in how we come out or whether we get out at all. In the example of Paul and Silas, we can find help for our midnight hour, for our time of testing, in an hour when the storms of life threaten to sweep us overboard. (See Acts 16:22-25)

When we confess the Word of God, the angels come, but when Praise and Worship in ministering to the Lord, He comes. According to Isaiah 43:25, "As they ministered to the Lord, and fasted, the Holy Ghost said... With hearts yielded to the Lord, full of love and praise.

F) The Holy Spirit and His Gifts

The Holy Spirit can manifest Himself and make known God's will and be leading us in a spiritual battle and give revelations via His gifts for according to 1 Corinthians 12:4-11. (See Psalm 22:3)

There are nine spiritual gifts of the Holy Spirit, these gifts are weapons that can be an aid to us as Christians because we are not wrestling with a natural enemy, but they are spirits.

List the Holy Spirit gifts of revelation: (gifts that reveal something)

- Gift of the Word of Wisdom, (specific instructions, future)
- Gift of the Word of Knowledge, (specific knowledge past or present)

- Gift of Discerning of Spirits, (specific knowledge of what type of spirit you are dealing with.)

List the Holy Spirit gifts of power.
- Gift of Faith, (special faith for the situation you are dealing with.)
- Gift of Healings, (special healing for the situation you are dealing with.)
- Gift of Working of Miracles, (Miracles for the situation you are dealing with.)

List the Holy Spirit gifts of utterance.
- Gift of Tongues, (supernatural utterance to God)
- Gift of Utterance, (supernatural revelations of what is being said by God)
- Gift of Prophecy, (supernatural words of encouragement from God, in a known language)

One of the gifts that are especially needed is the gift of discerning of spirits; this gift will give insight into what type of spirit you are dealing with. Another gift that is needed is the gift of the Word of Wisdom, specific wisdom of God on how to deal with the situation you are dealing with.

G) The Peace of God is a weapon

Jesus is called the Prince of Peace (See Isaiah 9:6-7). The Holy Spirit is the Spirit of Christ, the person of peace. Peace is like a double-edged sword: it is calming and magnificent for the believer, but very damaging and offensive toward the kingdom of darkness. "The God of peace will soon crush satan under your feet" (See Romans 16:20)

The Source of God's peace is God Himself. If fear knocks at the door, begin to face that fear with the God's peace come to the shepherd for restoration, for the reviving water and the tender green grass. Is it possible to have peace right in the middle of our chaotic lifestyle?

Peace, a weapon against the devil? If the devil cannot steal you Peace, he can move you to fear.

Summary

As God's children through faith in Jesus Christ, we receive a commission in God's army to continue the work of Christ in bringing every enemy under Christ's authority. Remember, whether your battle is public or private you will experience warfare, so get dressed, and with that in mind, we are given several instructions concerning readiness for battle. People who believe and obey Jesus Christ are among the most effective troops in God's army.

Chapter 11
The Law of Authority

We have the natural realm that is governed by laws and principles, and there is the realm of the spirit. The natural realm governs the law of gravity, the laws of electricity, and the laws of aerodynamics. These laws control functions in the natural and the physical realm. In the same way, there are laws, which govern operations in the realm of the spirit.

Let us look briefly at a crucial spiritual law, which governs the operation of all beings in the realm of the spirit. This is necessary for grasping the principle of spiritual jurisdiction. This law is called the law of authority.

Romans 3:27 declares that there is a law of faith. This law of faith governs the use of power in the spirit world. Love is call the "royal law" in **James 2:8**.

Romans 8:2 we are introducing to the "law of the Spirit of Life in Christ Jesus" which supersedes the law of sin and death.

These are just a few of the laws, which govern the realm of the spirit. Just a reminder as one fails to recognize and adhere to the natural laws, God has designed, and will always, prove to be physically disastrous, so failure to recognize and adhere to the spiritual laws, which God has ordained, will prove to be spiritually disastrous.

Romans 13:1-5;

"Let every soul be subject unto the higher powers. For there is no power but of God: the powers that be are ordained of God. ² Whosoever therefore resisteth the power, resisteth the ordinance of God: and they that resist shall receive to themselves damnation. ³ For rulers are not a terror to good works, but to the evil. Wilt thou then not be afraid of the power? Do that which is good and thou shalt have praise of the same: ⁴ For he is the minister of God to thee for good. However, if thou do that which is evil, be afraid; for he beareth not the sword in vain: for he is the minister of God, a revenger to execute wrath upon him that doeth evil. ⁵ Wherefore ye must needs be subject, not only for wrath, but also for conscience sake.

We read Romans 13:1-5; in verses, one and two the word "power" is used several times. This English word "power" is translated from the Greek word "exousia." The word "exousia," however, should be translated "authority." Although authority and power work together, like a hand and glove, they must be recognized as distinctly in the realm of spiritual things.

Let us replace the word "power" with "authority" and take a more accurate look at Romans 13:1-2:

"Let every soul be subject unto the higher (authorities). For there is no (authority) but of God: the (authorities) that be are ordained of God. Whosoever therefore resisteth the (authority) resisteth the ordinance of God: and they that resist shall receive to themselves damnation." (Parentheses mine)

Romans 13:1-2 teaches about a crucial law, which not only governs operations in the natural realm, but also governs operations in the realm of the spirit. This law is the law of authority. There is a spiritual law that is ordained by God, called the law of authority.

God ordained the law of authority. He instituted it and every spiritual being, including ourselves, we must cooperate with it. This law controls the operation of every spirit being and must be recognized and obeyed.

This law of authority is one of the greatest keys to understanding and operating in the realm of the spirit, and that those who have trouble submitting to the law of authority will have a tough time being used of God. In recognizing the law of authority, we can begin to understand the significance of the principle of spiritual jurisdiction.

A. What is Spiritual Jurisdiction?

Jurisdiction can be defined as "a range of authority." <u>Range</u> means "scope, boundaries, limitations, or distance." <u>Authority</u> means "the right to command, enforce, or intervene in a matter." Jurisdiction, then, means the right to exercise authority within a specific region or territory.

Spiritual jurisdiction is, "the boundaries within which a spiritual being has the right to command, enforce, intervene or exercise power in the realm of the spirit." All spirit beings have a range or region within which they do have the right to exercise and enforce power.

Conversely, all spirit beings have boundaries outside which they do not have the right to exercise or enforce power. This is the law of spiritual jurisdiction.

God has a spiritual jurisdiction. Angels have a particular spiritual jurisdiction. Men, both saved and unsaved, have a spiritual jurisdiction. satan and his demonic cohorts have a specific spiritual jurisdiction.

The boundary lines of a specific spiritual jurisdiction may be geographic, as with cities, states, or even nations, but mainly these boundaries pertain to established laws in spiritual matters and spiritual offices. Spiritual Jurisdiction is the law of authority, which governs the operation of all beings in the realm of the spirit.

B. Three Authorities in One World

We must understand three spiritual authorities have rights to operate. These three authorities are God, satan, and man. Some picture the spirit realm as a crazy, haphazard, unorganized world where it is impossible to predict what is going to happen.

That, however, is not true. We see, no kingdom, no system, and no realm can function without levels of authority. There is a law of authority, rank, and order, in the spirit realm.
Every being in the spirit realm must operate within the restraints of its boundaries of authority. The realm of the spirit is a highly organized and structured world and is governed by the law of the spiritual jurisdiction.

Some boundaries and borders measure out the extent and limitations of authority of every being in the realm of the spirit, just as the natural realm has boundaries defining the range of police jurisdiction. God has outlined for Himself that He will not transgress! So, there are boundaries in the spirit realm that outline the range of authority of satan, of demons and angels, of the believer, of ministerial offices and anointings.

In the Godhead there, is rank and authority. Jesus submits to the Father, and the Holy Spirit submits to the Father and the Son (2 Corinthians 11:3).

God's angels have rank and order. Daniel chapter 10 speaks of chief angels and the higher angels. Michael and Gabriel are examples of such higher angels.
In God's kingdom, there are cherubim, seraphim, and a variety of different angles with different duties and assignments, and different levels of authority. None of them steps outside their level of authority or their rank.

The devil's kingdom is also governed by a highly organized and structured system of rank and order (see Ephesians 6:11-13). The law of authority governs the activities of his demonic forces.

If we are a student of the Bible, we will have already learned that there are rank and order in the Body of Christ. To bless God, we need to act like the army that God is calling us to be. We need to endure hardness, follow orders, submit to those over us in the Lord, and quit breaking rank!

Spiritual Jurisdiction, these three authorities: God, satan (represented by the demon police officers) and man (represented by the believer). A believer must recognize that there are extents and limitations to God's authority, to satan authority, and to the authority, which man has as a believer.

There is a jurisdiction within which God can bless us, but there is a jurisdiction within which God is unable to bless us. There is a jurisdiction within which demons had authority to harass us. Man, also has a jurisdiction, which is represented by our right to choose which authority man to submit. There were limitations and boundaries concerning all three of these authorities.

Failure to recognize that God, satan, and man all have established boundaries within which they have a right to operate and outside of which they do not will keep us from understanding why things happen as they do. We will not know why certain things happen to believers.

We will not know who is exercising authority and, therefore, will not know whom to resist or when to resist. We will not be able to recognize if God is doing something or if it is the devil. We will not understand when to take spiritual initiative and when to rest in faith.

We will not recognize that there are limitations even to God's ability to bless us. We will not understand why our legal authority in Christ seems, at times, seem to be short-circuited. This is why satan seems to be free to exercise his power. We must recognize the extent and limitations of the boundaries of God's authority. We need to know that outside certain boundaries. He cannot bless us.

However, we must also realize that within certain boundaries He can and will bless us. We must realize that satan has certain boundaries within which he can exercise authority. Within certain boundaries, he has authority to harass and torment.

As one learned we would discover from God's Word; we can step out and stay outside of satan boundaries where he and his demons must desist their maneuvers in our lives. We must also realize that there are boundary lines outside of which we, as believers, cannot exercise our authority. Within specified boundaries, however, we can exercise our rights and reign as kings in this life. Recognizing and operating within these laws of authority is one of the greatest keys to operating effectively in the realm of the spirit.

Chapter 12
Levels of authority in the realm of the spirit

There are levels of authority in the realm of the spirit. Every being must operate within the boundaries of their authority. When we understand the law of authority and recognize the prominent place it has in the realm of the spirit, we will begin to understand the critical principle of spiritual jurisdiction.

A. God's Jurisdiction

Psalm 78:41; "Yea, they turned back and tempted God, and limited the Holy One of Israel."

Is there anything that God cannot do? Are there any limitations to His power? Can anyone or anything stop His will from coming to pass? Many would answer these questions with a confident, "NO!" However, as one read the Word of God, the answer is both yes and no. Though in one sense God is unlimited in His power and can do anything, it is also true that He has placed some limitations upon His operations in the life of humanity. For example:

Hebrews 6:18 says that it is impossible for God to lie.

James 1:13 says that God cannot be tempted with evil. Yes, God is all-powerful, but there are limitations He has placed upon Himself that we must understand.

We see, although God is omnipotent and sovereign, He has placed limitations upon Himself in this dispensation, especially in respect to His relationship with humanity.

It is essential that we discern between God's actual power, and His inherent power (i.e., His omnipotence, His omniscience, His omnipresence), and the power He can demonstrate based upon limitations He has established for Himself. For us to cooperate with God and receive His blessings, we must understand legal jurisdictions and know our responsibilities within these jurisdictions.

B. God's Jurisdiction and His Will

In **Luke 15:11-32**. In this story, the youngest son forfeited the blessings of his father by leaving father's house and going to foreign lands. In these faraway lands, he lost his inheritance and became a servant to a farmer, eating pig food.

At the point of total despair, he was wise enough to return to his father's house knowing that at least his father would take him back as a servant and he would be fed and clothed.

By simply walking in the works of the flesh as stated in Galatians five, you will find yourself outside of the jurisdiction of God (where He has the right to bless you) and inside the jurisdiction of satan (where he and his cohorts have the legal right to attack you'.

The prodigal son forfeited his blessings when he walked out of his father's house. Staying "in the house" — inside the boundaries of the will of God — will keep you in the place where the blessings of God can flow. Leaving "the house" — exiting the boundaries of the will of God will separate you from the power of God and limit His blessings in your life. Only when we come within the jurisdiction of the will of God can we receive God's blessings. It was only as we drew nigh to Him that He is able to draw nigh to me (James 4:7-8).

In Hebrews 1:9, we see the positive results of staying within the jurisdiction of the will of God. Reading and hear what the Word of God says concerning the Lord Jesus: "Thou hast loved righteousness (God's jurisdiction), and hated iniquity (satan jurisdiction); therefore God, even thy God, hath anointed thee with the oil of gladness above thy fellows." (Parentheses mine) Hebrews 1:9

Jesus lived within the boundaries of the perfect will of God, and, therefore, experiencing the full measure of the blessings of God. He was not anointed with the oil of gladness just because He was the Son of God. He was anointed with the oil of gladness because He loved righteousness. His measure of blessing was "above His fellows" because He loved righteousness and hated sin. He was blessed because He stayed within the boundaries of the perfect will of God.

God desires to bless us. He has things laid up for us. Ephesians 2:10 states that the Lord has prepared paths ahead of us; paths He has "... before ordained that we should walk in them." Nevertheless, when we wander outside of His will, we exit His jurisdiction, thus hindering Him from blessing us.

There is, a good, an acceptable and a perfect will of God (Romans 12:2). If one is only operating within the "good will" of God, then you are probably crossing back and forth between God's jurisdiction and the devil's jurisdiction. When we operate in this manner, we will wander in and out of the blessings of God and in and out of the harassment of the devil.

That is a dangerous lifestyle for a believer, and yet this is the way many believers live. When we live within the borders of God's perfect will, and within His jurisdiction. When we stay within the boundaries of God's perfect will, He can bless us as He wants to and we will "keep ourselves" from the power of satan.

In his book "Plans, Purposes, and Pursuits" Brother Kenneth E. Hagin recalls that the Lord spoke to him one time and said, "I bless all of my people as far as I can. Nevertheless, the reason there is not the move of God and the depth of the flow of the Spirit, and the fullness of the manifestation of the Holy Ghost today is because men do not take time to listen. They do not take time to follow God plans outlined in the scriptures. The more closely we follow His plan (Holy Spirit), the more my power will be in demonstration and manifestation" (underline mine).

One reason that some believers are not receiving the blessings of God. It is not that blessings do not belong to us in Christ. It is not that God does not desire to bless us.

It is because we have submitted two works of the flesh rather than to the will of God. It is because we either have not listened to God's plan or have not carefully followed what we know to be His plan. In so doing, we have put ourselves "across the border" from the jurisdiction of God.

We have limited God and forfeited His blessings by operating outside His will. Jesus is Lord within His jurisdiction, but He cannot bless us when we "walk" outside His jurisdiction.

He cannot bless us fully of His desires if we are outside the boundaries of His perfect will. God's will for Christians life, not only includes the specific instructions of His written word, but also His plan for Christians life, His call upon Christians life and His assignments to Christians in life.

God wants to bless us all. He wants to meet our needs. We must live within the boundaries of His power and authority. We must get out of the territory of the works of the flesh. We must get out of the territory of doing our things our ways and enter into the territory of God. We must enter into the territory of His perfect will for our lives, by not being in the proper territory humanity can block the blessing of God. Get out of the devil's jurisdiction and into God's jurisdiction. We will find that the harassment of demonic spirits will be broken off from over Christians life and they will cross over into the "land of milk and honey," the territory where the blessings of God always flow!

C. God's Jurisdiction and His Word

We must walk within the boundaries of God's will to live safely and receive the blessings of His jurisdiction. What is God's will? However, the specific aspects of God's will for our lives can only be discovered by spending time in prayer and by following the Holy Ghost, the most fundamental aspects of God's will is His record in His Word!

To abide within the blessed borders of God's jurisdiction and experience His great blessings, one must live within the boundaries of His Word.

God's blessings have always been tied to this condition of walking within the boundary lines of His Word. Believers who expect to experience the blessings of the Christian life without meeting the conditions of the Christian life are ignorant of the Bible and the operation of spiritual laws. We see it is not a matter of whether God wants to bless us or not. The fact of the matter is that God cannot bless us if we live outside of obedience to His Word. Repeatedly the Lord places the condition of obedience upon the receiving of our needs and the fulfillment of our desires.

Deuteronomy 28:1-2 says,

"And it shall come to pass, if thou shalt hearken diligently unto the voice of the Lord thy God, to observe and to do all his commandments which I command thee this day, that the Lord thy God will set thee on high above all nations of the earth: And all these blessings shall come on thee, and overtake thee, if thou shalt hearken unto the voice of the Lord thy God."

Joshua 1:8 says,

"This book of the law shall not depart out of thy mouth; but thou shalt meditate therein day and night, that thou mayest observe to do according to all that is written therein: for then thou shalt make thy way prosperous, and then thou shalt have good success."

To abide within the scope of God's blessings, one must abide within the boundaries of the teachings of His Word.

D. God's Jurisdiction and Man's Will

We know that the Lord is sovereign. In His sovereignty, He has chosen to limit Himself in His dealings with man. He has limited Himself by giving man a will and, therefore, the freedom to choose whether to cooperate with Him and His Word. He has also designed that most of His operations in the earth would be through the agency of man. (See Amos 3:7)

In His dealings with humanity, primarily as concerns His desire to bless, God will never violate the human will. Though he desires that all men be saved (1 Timothy 2:4 and 2 Peter 3:9).

God will never force anyone to be saved. Though He has the power to rescue and liberate those held captive to sin, and though He has the power to unshackle the prisoners of darkness, He cannot do so until they call upon His name. He cannot rescue those bound by satan rule if they choose to continue to live there. Again, God can, not because in His omnipotent sovereignty He gave man a will (the right to choose) and has placed that as a limitation over His dealings in our lives.

Only then could Jesus say, "Go thy way; thy faith hath made thee whole." This reality is clearly demonstrated in the ministry of Jesus. In John 5:1-9 we read the story of Jesus healing a man who had an infirmity for 38 years.

Before He could heal the man, Jesus had to ask, "Wilt thou be made whole?" Jesus, the Son of God, God in the flesh, had to find out if the man wanted to be healed before He could heal him.

He had to know the man's will. The man clarified to Jesus that it was, in fact, his will to be healed by reporting that each time the water of the pool was stirred, he tried to get in, but someone always got in before he could. After ascertaining the will of this impotent man Jesus said, "Rise, take up thy bed, and walk."

In Mark 10:46-52 we find the story of blind Bartimaeus. After Jesus called Bartimaeus to himself, he asked him, "What wilt thou that I should do unto thee?" He needed to find out what Bartimaeus wanted even though he knew what Bartimaeus needed. He needed to know Bartimaeus' will concerning his condition. Bartimaeus permitted Jesus to heal him by telling him that he wanted to receive his sight.

The reality that God will not violate the human will is also seen in the calling of God upon people's lives. He never forces His will on people, but merely invites them to "follow Me." After He makes this invitation, it is up to each person to submit his or her will to His will. Even Jesus, who ministered as a human being, had to submit His will to the Father for the power of God to flow through His life and the plan of God to be accomplished through His death.

1. God Has Chosen to move through Man

For us to understand God's jurisdiction in this physical realm, we must recognize the authority, which he delegated to man. In the beginning, God delegated unto Adam an exclusive authority in this physical world.

In so doing, He granted unto humanity a jurisdiction within which he had the right to rule. Though Adam yielded up a part of that authority to the devil in the Garden of Eden, it is still necessary to have a physical body to exercise authority in the earth.

We see, there is a strong relationship between authority in this earth and having a physical body. For God's power and authority to be maximized to its fullest potential in the earth, it must flow through the clay-based vessel of a man, a physical body. The devil desires to possess and control men's lives today. It is so that he can exercise his authority in the earth using their bodies.

As one studies God's Word, he will discover that the omnipotent God of the Universe has chosen to limit Himself to working through the agency of man. In support of this, we find specific scriptures such as **Ezekiel 22:29-31**, which teaches us that in His overall blueprint of the ages, God has chosen to limit His right to deliver men through the prayers of a man.

Romans 5:12-21 is very clear that it was through a man that our redemption from sin had to come.

"The people of the land have used oppression, and exercised robbery, and have vexed the poor and needy: yea, they have oppressed the stranger wrongfully. And I sought for a man among them, that should make up the hedge, and stand in the gap before me for the land, that I should not destroy it: but I found none."

Romans 5:15, 19

"Much more the grace of God, and the gift by grace, which is by one man, Jesus Christ, hath abounded unto many... by the obedience of one (man) shall many be made righteous"

The mystery of godliness as Paul declared in 1 Timothy 3:16. God had to become a man to exercise His power and authority in the earth and bring redemption to humanity.

From these and other scriptures, we understand that God has to have a vehicle, as it were, to move through in this physical world.

That vehicle is a man. For in this earth realm God has delegated authority to man, and He will not violate nor alter that which He has spoken out of His mouth (Psalms 89:34). Therefore, God will continue to operate and perform His will on this earth through the vessel of humanity until the time, as we know it is no more and His plan is complete! This reality is another boundary, which defines God's jurisdiction.

E. God's Jurisdiction and Faith

A final condition that acts as a border in defining God's limitations and extends to bless is the border of faith. James 1:6-7 and Hebrews 11:6 points this out.

James 1: 6-7 says this concerning our receiving the blessings of God: "6 But let him ask in faith, nothing wavering. For he that wavereth is like a wave of the sea driven with the wind and tossed. 7 For let not that man think that he shall receive any thing of the Lord."

God cannot and will not move outside the boundary line of faith. Not only is it impossible to please God without faith, as Hebrews 11:6 declare, but one will limit God from working in his life without faith.

In Psalms 78:41, we read about how the children of Israel, through doubt, hindered God from blessing their lives, "Yea, they turned back and tempted God, and limited the Holy One of Israel."

God was limited by the lack of faith of the children of Israel. Because they failed to mix faith with God's Word, He could not take them into the promised land of Canaan (Hebrews 4:1-2). Hebrews 3:19 makes this truth, "So we see that they could not enter in because of unbelief."

It was not a matter of God's desire to bless Israel that kept them out of the Promised Land. It was a matter of them not believing what He had spoken. He could not fulfill His declared will and purpose without their cooperation by faith.

Matthew 13:58 says of Jesus that,

"Jesus did no mighty works there (in Nazareth) because of their unbelief." Mark's gospel says that He, "... could there do no mighty work" (Mark 6:5).

This was not a matter of Jesus' will to heal the sick in Nazareth. It was a matter of His limitations to bless people outside of the boundary line of their faith. God is the Almighty, all-sufficient God of the universe. However, He has placed borders and limitations upon the use of His power and upon the outpouring of His blessings.

If the believer ignores this reality, it will not only cost him many of the benefits of his covenant with God but may also lead him to the place where he points an accusing finger at God.

If we are not walking in the blessings that God has promised in His Word, it is because we have not positioned our lives in that place where God can use His power to bless and to save.

Recognize that there is a range of authority that defines God's power to bless and place yourself within the jurisdiction of His power and love.

Summary

Understanding that God has established borders, which define and limit His exercise of authority in this physical realm helps explain why things happen to believers and why, though we have many promises of God, we seem to experience a low level of blessing in our daily lives. God will not transgress the borders of His jurisdiction. These borders are the borders of His Word, the border of His will, the border of man's will, and the border of faith.

Chapter 13
The Believer's Jurisdiction

It is essential that we as believers must understand our legal authority over satan and his host. It is just as important, however, that we understand how to exercise that authority. What good is it to us if we know we are free from satan power but do not know how to appropriate our freedom? See, for every truth of God's Word, there is a legal side and a practical side. There is the specific truth, but there is also the practical aspect of walking in that truth.

In understanding the Authority of the Believer, emphasizing the practical application of this reality and exploring how our authority relates to the principle of spiritual jurisdiction.

A. Our Legal Position of Authority

In Ephesians chapters, one and two we learn about the legal authority of the believer. **Ephesians 1:19-21** reveals that God has positioned His Son in a place of preeminence and power.

> "... *according to the working of his mighty power, Which he wrought in Christ, when he raised him from the dead, and set him at his own right hand in the heavenly places, Far above all principality, and power, and might, and dominion, and every name that is named, not only in this world, but also in that which is to come:*"

Here we learn that Jesus is position in the highest place of spiritual authority. He is seated over all the powers of the enemy. As we proceed to Ephesians chapter, two we discover a marvelous truth concerning our spiritual position.

Not only has God raised Jesus from the dead and positioned Him in a place of authority, but He has also raised us up from the dead and positioned us with Christ in that same place of authority.

> **Ephesians 2:4-6;**
>
> *"But God, who is rich in mercy, for his great love wherewith he loved us, Even when we were dead in sins, hath quickened us together with Christ, (by grace ye are saved;) And hath raised us up together, and made us sit together in heavenly places in Christ Jesus:"*

Our position in Christ is "far above all principality, and power, and might, and dominion..." **(Ephesians 1:21)**. Through our identification with Christ, we have the same legal authority over the devil that Jesus has! That is what **1 John 4:17** says as it declares "... as He (Jesus) is, so are we in this world."

We must remember, however, that the exercise of every being's authority is limited by the boundaries of its jurisdiction. Only within certain boundaries can the believer exercise his authority.

Outside of these boundaries, he cannot exercise authority. The authority of the believer has limitations that must be recognized.

Let us identify some of the boundaries, which determine the extent, and limitations of the believer's authority.

1) The Boundary of the Spirit Realm

The scriptures reveal a very important boundary that governs our authority as believers.

> **2 Corinthians 10:3-4**
>
> *"For though we walk in the flesh, we do not war after the flesh: For the weapons of our warfare are not carnal, but mighty through God to the pulling down of strongholds..."*

The true jurisdiction of the believer is in the realm of the spirit, for our authority is not a natural authority, but a spiritual authority.

Our authority is not in the natural realm! Though our authority can be used to change circumstances in the physical realm, it is not from the physical realm that we operate or exercise our intervention. Our spiritual authority is exercise from our position in Christ. By using the weapons of preaching, prayer, confession, and other spiritual weapons, we fight our good fight of faith. Continuing to verse four we read, "For the weapons of our warfare are not carnal..." If the weapons of our warfare are not carnal, then they must be spiritual!

To war after the flesh is to war outside the range of our authority, when we step outside the jurisdiction of our authority when we resort to the natural weaponry of carnal man! Nevertheless, when we remain in that territory called the realm of the spirit, we can exercise our right to intervene in the matters of this world.

2) The Boundary of Faith

The authority of the believer will not successfully operate outside the boundaries of faith. In the gospel of Matthew, we find an account that illustrates this point.

Matthew 17:14-20a;

"And when they were come to the multitude, there came to him a certain man, kneeling down to him, and saying, Lord, have mercy on my son: for he is a lunatick, and sore vexed: for oft times he falleth into the fire, and oft into the water. And I brought him to thy disciples, and they could not cure him. Then Jesus answered and said, O faithless and perverse generation, how long shall I be with you? How long shall I suffer you? Bring him hither to me. And Jesus rebuked the devil; and he departed out of him: and the child was cured from that very hour. Then came the disciples to Jesus apart, and said, why could not we cast him out? And Jesus said unto them, Because of your unbelief..."

Jesus had already delegated to the disciples' authority to cast out devils. However, this delegated authority would not function outside the boundary of faith. Only a few weeks before Jesus had empowered the twelve with "... power over unclean spirits, to cast them out..." (Matthew 10:11, they failed to exercise their authority because they operated outside the boundary of faith.

The fact that their authority over this particular demonic spirit was limited was a great surprise to these twelve men. Upon questioning Jesus, however, they discovered that their delegated authority would not operate outside the boundary of faith.

This account in Matthew reminder of a story that Brother Kenneth E. Hagin tells in his book "I Believe in Visions," in the chapter, "If — the Badge of Doubt." In this chapter, Brother Hagin recalls an instance in the early days of his healing ministry when he was attempting to cast a devil out of a man who had tuberculosis of the spine.

After he cast the devil out of the sick man, Brother Hagin said to the man, "See if you can stoop over and bend your back." Brother Hagin recalls that as long as he asked the man to "See if you can..." the man could not. Jesus appeared to brother Hagin at this time and instructed him concerning this situation. Following this vision, he corrected and commanded the man to bend over in the name of Jesus. The man obeyed and was instantly healed. Brother Hagin concluded that chapter of his book by saying,

"I learned that no matter who we are, if we move in unbelief, we will stop the flow of God's power."

This story to illustrate the fact that our authority as believers will not operate outside the boundary line of faith. Another way of expressing this truth is to say that we negate our authority when we step outside the boundary line of faith.

Our authority over satan can only be exerted when we operate within the borderlines of God's Word. Even in the ministry of deliverance, if satan can get believers on his "turf" through unbelief, or if you go past the directions of God's Word, then you will not be able to cast out devils even though you have the legal authority to do so!

For example, those who try to cast devils out and command them to go to hell, or try to cast them into the abyss or the lake of fire, will not be able to minister deliverance to the captives. That person is trying to operate their authority outside the boundaries of God's written Word. Nowhere does the Bible say that we can cast demons back into hell, or into the abyss or the lake of fire. No, the Bible plainly says that we should cast demons. That is all we need to do.

Any time the devil can seduce us or deceive us over the boundary line of God's Word, our authority over him will be less effective, and his operations will remain intact. Therefore, let us remain in the Word and, thereby, maintain our full authority as believers.

Summary

There are boundary lines and limiting borders that define the range of authority or spiritual jurisdiction; we have as believers.

The boundaries of the realm of the spirit, of faith, and of the Word of God are the boundaries that define our jurisdiction. We must abide within these boundaries, and we can expect to walk in the level of power that has been legally provided for us within these boundaries.

When believers transgress these boundary lines and leave the borders of our authority, we lose power in our lives and experience a breakdown in the real authority purchased for us by God. However, remaining within the boundary lines of our spiritual jurisdiction will enable us to appropriate the authority that does belong to us as believers.

Chapter 14
The devil Jurisdiction

People are often unaware that satan has authority in this world. There is, however, a domain within which he has the right to exercise his power. This domain is known as the devil kingdom and in his kingdom; he has the right to enforce his power. Another way of expressing this truth is just to say that satan has a spiritual jurisdiction. He has a realm within which he has the right to enforce his will.

2 Corinthians 4:4;

"In whom the god of this world hath blinded the minds of them which believe not, lest the light of the glorious gospel of Christ, who is the image of God, should shine unto them."

It is crucial that believers recognize and define the devil jurisdiction. In this way, they can avoid the deceptive devices he uses against them. Knowing the boundaries of the devil authority will keep believers from falling into the pitfalls and traps that he spreads before the feet of God's people.

A. Defining the devil Kingdom and his jurisdiction

When Adam yielded himself to sin in the Garden of Eden, he transferred to satan the jurisdiction, which God had entrusted to man. Through Adam's fall, satan gained the right to operate upon this earth and gained legal authority over people. He established a kingdom and an operating system and took the place of spiritual jurisdiction in this world.

He is the ruler of the kingdoms of this world, the ruler over demonic entities, and the ruler over those who have not been translated out from under his authority through the work of Christ. Jesus confirmed this reality on several occasions. In John 12:31 and in John 16:11 Jesus called satan the "prince (or ruler) of this world." Besides, in Matthew 12:26 Jesus revealed that satan has a kingdom by saying.

> **Matthew 12:26**
> *"... if satan cast out satan, he is divided against himself; how then shall his kingdom stand?"*

The devil himself claimed jurisdiction and revealed how he came to possess it. In Luke 4:6, he told Jesus that the kingdoms of this world had been delivered to him and that, "... to whomsoever, I will I give it."

The devil's kingdom is not the planet called earth, but rather the world, or this world system. The earth is the Lord's and the fullness thereof. This world system, dominated by the powers of greed and lust, is the devil domain. In II Corinthians 4:4, he is called, "... the god of this world..." This scripture is clear and strong. By calling satan, "god," the Bible signifies that he has authority. Also, by calling him the god of "this world" the Word of God clarifies that there is a particular realm in which he has authority.

We must define the extents and limitations of his right to operate. We must define what he has a legal right to do and what he does not have a legal right to do. We must clearly define his kingdom and mark the borders of his legal jurisdiction. How can we identify the devil kingdom? How can we locate the boundaries of his jurisdiction?

The devil kingdom cannot be defined by geographical boundaries or by any visible natural borders. These two ways can define it:

1. By identifying those over whom he can legally exercise authority.
2. By defining the forces that govern the world system in which he is lord.

First, let us consider the boundaries of the devil jurisdiction by asking the question, "Over whom can satan exercise authority?" The answer to this question, we will see that satan has different rights relative to demons, unbelievers, and believers.

Concerning demonic forces, satan has unlimited authority because they chose to obey him in the heavenly insurrection. The devil right to use his authority extends over all the demons, which fell with him from heaven. He is called the prince of the authority of the air (See Ephesians 2:2).

The word "air" signifies that sphere in which the demonic forces operate (Vine's). He is, then, the "Archon" (Greek), or ruler, of that sphere in which demonic forces operate. The New English Bible calls him, "the commander of the spiritual powers of the air..." satan is chief of and has full authority over all demonic entities.
The whole demonic kingdom falls under his jurisdiction. satan also has jurisdiction over some people. He has the authority through the law of sin and death (See Romans 8:2) overall unsaved people.

Ephesians 2:2 he is called,

> "... *The spirit that now worketh in the children of disobedience.*"

Those who are in rebellion to God, not those born again, are under the devil jurisdiction and rulership. Ephesians 6:12 says that satan is the "ruler of the darkness of this world." Within this world system with its lust and darkness, satan is "god." He has the authority and, therefore, power over the citizens that choose to inhabit the spiritual territory called "this world."

The devil rights concerning the unbeliever are almost limitless. He is the unbeliever's god and father, and they are all legal subjects of his kingdom. He has the right to blind them and bind them up in his chains and fetters of sin and death.

Concerning the believer, however, satan only has certain limited rights. These rights differ from his rights with unbelievers, and with demons.

1. satan has the right to tempt, test and confront (Ephesians 6:13, 16).
2. satan has the right to *attempt* physical attack.
3. satan has the right to *attempt* to plant thoughts in our mind (John 13:2; Acts 5:3).
4. satan has the right to roam about throughout the earth and *attempt* to devour (1 Peter 5:8).
5. satan and has the right to *attempt* control and deception (1 Timothy 4:1).
6. He can *attempt* to wield power and influence over us.
7. He has the right to give the kingdoms of this world to whomsoever he will (Luke 4:6).

8. He has the right to accuse the brethren (Revelation 12:10).
9. satan can also *attempt* to bring upon the believer other works of his kingdom.
10. He can attempt to inflict sickness, fear, poverty, depression, lust, hate, greed, and division.

The reason satan has the right to attempt to inflict the believer in these various ways is that we share this planet with him. Note again, however, that satan does not have the right to devour, only the right to attempt to devour.
He can only challenge our authority in Christ. The believer determines any further rights satan may have beyond the right to challenge.

His limitations concerning the believer can also define the devil jurisdiction. satan does not have the right to stay when resisted by the believer James 4:7). satan does not have the right to make the believer sin (Romans 6:13).
He cannot tempt us beyond what we can resist (1 Corinthians 10:13). He does not have the right to separate us from the love of God, which is in Christ Jesus (Romans 8:38-39). satan cannot steal our salvation (John 10:28-29).

B. Jurisdiction over these three groups of beings:

1. satan has certain rights to enforce his power. Demons, unsaved individuals, and believers

2. The devil kingdom can be recognized by the forces that operate within his sphere of influence. These forces include fear, strife, rebellion, disobedience, pride, and many other lusts.

3. When an individual, saved or unsaved, is walking under the influence of these forces, they are surely walking in the devil's territory, well within his jurisdiction.

The boundaries of the devil jurisdiction in this world system are also defined by time. In the account of the Gadarene demoniac, the demon in control asked Jesus the question, "... art thou come hither to torment us before the time?" (Matthew 8:29) The devil duration of operation extends from the time of Adam's transgression until he is bound up during the millennial reign of Jesus Christ for a thousand years.

After one-thousand-year period, he will be loosed and will have jurisdiction for another short period. Finally, he will be judged and eternally bound, and his jurisdiction will cease forever. Hallelujah! (See Revelation 20:1-10).

The devil jurisdiction includes his control over demons, his deceptive power to blind the unsaved, and his right to attempt to enforce his power over the believer. Within this world system, over certain classes of people, and for a specific length of time satan can rightfully exercise his power. All these extents and limitations mark the borders of the devil jurisdiction.

B. We 'believers' have been legally delivered from the devil jurisdiction.

Remembering that the definition of jurisdiction is, "the range of authority" or "the boundaries within which authority can be exercised" we can see a fresh new picture of what **Colossians 1:13** is teaching.

Colossians 1:13

"Who hath delivered us from the power (authority) of darkness, and hath translated us into the kingdom of his dear Son:"

Legally satan has no more right to enforce power over you than would a North Carolina sheriff in a Chesterfield County, Virginia. Although the North Carolina sheriff has a badge and a gun (he has power), he does not have the authority to use it outside the boundaries of his jurisdiction.

As believers, we have been delivered from the devil's authority. Colossians 1:13 declares, "Who (God) hath delivered us from the power ("exousia" — authority or jurisdiction) of darkness, and hath translated us into the kingdom (or jurisdiction) of His Dear Son." In this scripture, we again find that the Greek word "exousia" has been translated "power." However, "exousia" means an authority or jurisdiction. Believers have been delivered out of the jurisdiction of darkness and translated into the jurisdiction of God!

Here in the midst of the reality of our redemption, we find the law of spiritual jurisdiction. The blood of Jesus and through His death, burial, and resurrection has translated us out of the devil kingdom into God's. We have been transferred out of the realm where legal authority has and become citizens of God's domain.

The word "translated" in Colossians 1:13 comes from two Greek words which mean change" and "to stand." We were standing in the kingdom of darkness under the devil authority, but our place of standing has changed.

We have been brought out of his kingdom and have been made to stand strong and secure in God's kingdom!

We have been delivered out of the realm where the devil has authority in the region where Jesus is Lord! We have been transported out of the devil range! In fact, you could translate this verse by saying that, "We have been translated out of the devil's jurisdiction into God's jurisdiction!"

(1) Seated in Heavenly Places (Positional)

Legally we are out of the devil's range. We have been seated in heavenly places in Christ Jesus through God's redemptive plan.

Ephesians 1:21 tells us that Jesus is positioned "far above all principality and power ("exousia"; authority or jurisdiction) and might and dominion..."

Ephesians 2:6 says that God has also raised us up together and made us sit together in heavenly places in Christ Jesus. We have been raised up out of the devil range!

Legally satan has no more right to enforce power over you than would a North Carolina sheriff in a Chesterfield County, Virginia. Although the North Carolina sheriff has a badge and a gun (he has power), he does not have the authority to use it outside the boundaries of his jurisdiction.

Though we are legally free from the devil jurisdiction, however, living in the reality of our redemptive position in Christ Jesus is another thing altogether. Living daily in our place of liberty from the devil authority is where the "rubber meets the road."

One of the greatest lessons we can learn concerning the law of spiritual jurisdiction. We can learn how to stay out of the devil range and how to walk in freedom from his authority.

Chapter 15
Starting Your Day, A Warfare Prayer and Armor of God

Ephesians 6:18 "Praying always with all prayer"
1 Corinthians 14:40 "done decently and in order"

A. Worship Our Heavenly Father:

Heavenly Father, I come to you in the name of Jesus, and I thank you for the guidance of the Holy Spirit. I enter your gates with thanksgiving and present an offering of thanks. I enter your court with praise! I am thankful and delight to say so. I bless and praise your name! For you are good and your mercy and loving kindness are everlasting. Your faithfulness and truth endure to all generations. It is a good delightful thing to give thanks to You O Most High. I thank you for what you are doing in my life. (Jeremiah 29:11 (NIV); for I know the plans I have for you," declares the LORD, "plans to prosper you and not to harm you, plans to give you hope and a future.) Quote Psalms 100

(1) ENTER INTO HIS GATES WITH THANKSGIVING: (EXAMPLE)

Heavenly Father, I thank you for the manifestation of what I believe that I receive: (Mark 11:22-23); You can make lists of the things that you believe God for and give thanks each day until they have manifested. In addition, each day you are to bind the devil from blocking the manifestation of what you are believing God for.

On a consistent basis In the Name of Jesus, I bind that devil and all his cohorts from hindering the manifestation of what I believe that I receive, and I release your holy angels on my behalf causing the things that I believe that I receive to be manifested.

Heavenly Father, I enter into his courts with praise: I Praise You for what you have done in my life (Only you know What God has done personally in your life).

Heavenly Father, I thank you that I can enter into your gates with thanksgiving, and enter into your courts with praise, but I count it a blessing to come before his presence with singing. I bow in worship because of who you are. I thank You for allowing me to come and fellowship with an open heart to heart relationship with you as your (son/daughter) through the Lord Jesus Christ.

HEAVEN FATHER, I BOW IN WORSHIP BEFORE YOU BECAUSE OF WHO YOU ARE:

1. EL-Elyon the "Most High God" (Genesis 14:17-20;
2. Psalm 91:2-4, Jeremiah 32:38-40, Isaiah 14:13-14, and Psalms 21:7)
3. EL-Gmulot the "The Lord Who Rewards" Jeremiah 32:18, 51:56, Romans 12:17-19 2 Thessalonians 1:6, Hebrews 10:30)
4. EL-Olam the "Everlasting God" (Isaiah 40:28-31)
5. EL-Roi "God of sight who keeps watch" (Genesis 16:13)
6. EL-Shaddai the "God, that's more than enough", the All sufficient one" (Genesis 17:1 and Psalm 91:1)
7. ELOHIM the "God that creates" (Genesis 1:1, Psalms 19:1)
8. ADONAI the "Master and owner of everything" (Psalms 24:1, Malachi 1:6)

YOU ARE JEHOVAH THE LORD, GOD, WHICH REVEALETH:

1. JEHOVAH "Unchangeable, "Intimate God" (Isaiah 45:21, Psalm 139:1-5)
2. JEHOVAH-YAHWEH "The God's of divine salvation" (Genesis 3:15, Romans 10:9-10),
3. JEHOVAH-TSIDKENU "The Lord our righteousness" (Jeremiah 23:5-6, 1 Corinthians 1:30),
4. JEHOVAH-MACCADDESH "The Lord our Sanctifier" (Exodus 31:13, Psalm 90:17, 1 Corinthian 1:30, 2 Peter 1:4)
5. JEHOVAH-SHALOM "Our Peace and Wholeness (Judges 6:24, Matthew 11:28-29, John 14:27)
6. JEHOVAH-SHAMMAH "The Lord who is Present" (Ezekiel 48:35; Psalm 16:9, 11, Matthew 28:19-20, Hebrews 13:5,8),
7. JEHOVAH-RAPHA "The Lord our healer" (Exodus 15:26, Isaiah 53:5, Jeremiah 30:1 Peter 2:24),
8. JEHOVAH-TSEBAOTH "To wage war/ to render service to God" Genesis 2:1, Psalm 147:4, Joshua 10:12)
9. JEHOVAH-JIREH "The Lord our provide" (Genesis 22:13-14, Philippians 4:19),
10. JEHOVAH-NISSI "The Lord our banner, Lord You reign in victory"(Exodus 17:15, Romans 8:37, 1 Corinthians 15:57),
11. JEHOVAH-SABAOTH "The Lord of Hosts" (Isaiah 6:1-3, Romans 9:29, James 5:4),
12. EHOVAH-ROHI "The Lord our shepherd" (Psalm 23:1-6, John 10:14-16, Hebrews 13:20-21)

(2) LORD JESUS CHRIST

Lord Jesus, as my Lord and Savior, I thank you because you are seated at the right hand of my **Heavenly Father,** as my High Priest interceding on my behalf. I thank you for receiving my tithes and offerings and worshiping my Heavenly Father with them.

LORD JESUS, I PRAISE YOU LORD JESUS, because OF YOU: I am saved by grace. I am a son of God. Your precious blood has redeemed me. I am a new creature. I am born-again. I am born of incorruptible seed. I am a partaker of God's divine nature. I am a member of a chosen generation. I am more than a conqueror. I am a citizen of the kingdom of heaven. I am seated in heavenly places in you. I am fearfully and wonderfully made. I am an ambassador for You Lord Jesus. I am abounding in a spirit of thanksgiving. I am redeemed from the curse of the law. I am forgiven of all my sins. Lord Jesus, I Praise You and thank you that I am fathered from above. I am accepted in the Beloved; I am the righteousness of God. I am the light of the world. I am a part of the royal priesthood. I am an heir of God and I am a joint heir with You Lord Jesus. I am covered with Your precious Blood, I praise YOU for your WORDs.

> **Hebrews 11:6;**
> *"But without faith it is impossible to please him: for he that cometh to God must believe that he is, and that he is a rewarder of them that diligently seek him."*
>
> **Luke 10:19,**
> *"Behold, I give unto You authority (power) over all the ability (power) of the enemy, and nothing by any means shall hurt me."*

Matthew 18:18-19;

"You said... "Verily I say unto you, whatsoever ye shall bind on earth shall be bound in heaven: and whatsoever ye shall loose on earth shall be loosed in Heaven. Again I say unto you, that if two of you shall agree on earth as touching anything that they shall ask, it shall be done for them of my Father which is in heaven."

Mark 11:22-23,

"You said ..." And Jesus answering saith unto them, have faith in God. For verily I say unto you, That whosoever shall say unto this mountain, be thou removed, and be thou cast into the sea; and shall not doubt in his heart, but shall believe that those things which he saith shall come to pass, he shall have whatsoever he saith."

John 20:17;

"You said... Jesus saith unto her, Touch me not, for I am not yet ascended to my Father, but go to my brethren, and say unto them, I ascend unto my Father, and your Father; and to my God, and your God.

1 Corinthians 2:4-5;

"And my speech and my preaching were not with persuasive words of human wisdom, but in demonstration of the Spirit and of power, that your faith should not be in the wisdom of men but in the power of God.

Lord Jesus, You are my Lord and Savior and I thank You for allowing me to Fellowship (friend ship/camaraderie/companionship) with You today. Lord Jesus, I bow in worship before You because you are "Worthy as the Lamb of God that was slain to receive power, riches, wisdom, strength, honor, glory, and blessings. (Revelation 5:12)

LORD JESUS, I BOW IN WORSHIP BEFORE YOU BECAUSE OF WHO YOU ARE:

1. Emmanuel "God with us" (Matthew 1:23)
2. Only Potentate, the King of kings, and Lord of lords (Revelation 17:14, Revelation 19:16, 1 Timothy 6:15)
3. Messiah (Daniel 9:25, John 1:41, 4:25-26)
4. Wonderful Counselor (Isaiah 9:6)
5. Almighty (Revelation 1:8)
6. Everlasting Father (Isaiah 9:6, John 1:1-3)
7. Prince of Peace (Isaiah 9:6/John 14:27)
8. Redeemer (Job 19:25)
9. Son of God (Luke 1:35, John 9:37, John 10:36)
10. Lamb of God (John 1:29)
11. Lord of Glory (James 2:1)

(3) BLESSED HOLY SPIRIT:

Blessed Holy Spirit, I welcome your leading and guidance in my life, and I Thank You for my being sealed, sanctified and set apart by you. I will complete the work that you have called me to do.

Blessed Holy Spirit, I Thank You for giving me new ways of living and better strategies for life. I Thank You for upgrading me with kingdom technology and kingdom methodology, I Thank You for giving me the supernatural discipline to implement them; I Thank You for leading and guiding me into all truth; I Thank You for ordering my steps according to Your original plan and purpose for my life.

I Thank You for opening divine gates of access to new doors of opportunity. I Thank You for windows of divine inspiration. I Thank You for the insight, and revelation.

I Thank You for leading me in the paths of righteousness, and to avenues of success and prosperity; I Thank You for giving me multiple streams of income and positive cash flow; I Thank You for leading me on the highways to places of divine assignments and prosperity.

I Thank You for giving me insight and understanding that is not available through any other means, I Thank You for the keys to solving unsolvable challenges.

Blessed Holy Spirit, I Thank and Praise You for a fresh anointing, and help me to be a vessel that can be used by You, and that the Lord Jesus Christ be lifted up in my life, that Almighty God, my Heavenly Father be glorified in my life, and that the devil's defeat be demonstrated in my life.

I Thank and Praise You for the manifestation of your gifts according 1 Corinthians 12:4-10. "The gift of the word of wisdom. The gift of the word of knowledge, The gift of faith, The gift of healings, The gift of working of miracles, The gift of prophecy, The gift of discerning of spirits, The gift of the divers kinds of tongues, and interpretation of tongues". I Thank and Praise You for revealing mysteries and revelation knowledge.

Blessed Holy Spirit, I Praise You because You are the Spirit of Wisdom, You are the Spirit of Understanding, You are the Spirit Counsel, You are the Spirit of Might, You are the Spirit of knowledge, You are the Spirit of fear of the Lord, and I thank You for giving me prophetic insight.

Blessed Holy Spirit, You are my ever present companion and friend who just happens to be God; I thank you for allowing me to Partner with you to do Kingdom business.

BLESSED HOLY SPIRIT, I BOW IN WORSHIP BEFORE YOU BECAUSE WHO YOU ARE:

1. Spirit of Adoption (Galatians 4:6)
2. Spirit of Faith (2 Corinthians 4:13)
3. Spirit of Glory (1 Peter 4:14)
4. Spirit of Grace (Hebrews 10:29)
5. Spirit of Holiness (Romans 1:4)
6. Spirit of Judgment and burning (Isaiah 28:6)
7. Spirit of Power (Luke 24:49, Acts 1:8, 10:38, Romans 15:13, 2 Timothy 1:7)
8. Spirit of Prayer "Advocate – one who pray on behalf" Zechariah 12:10, Romans 8:26, 27, 1 Corinthians 14:15
9. Spirit of Truth (John 14:17)
10. Greater One who lives in me (1 John 4:4)
11. Reveal of Mysteries (1 Corinthians 2:6-12)
12. Comforter "Parakletos – one who is called alongside to help" (John 14:26, John 15:26)
13. Spiritual Guide (John 16:13, Romans 8:14)
14. Teacher (John 14:26)

Heavenly Father, I wait on you this day __/__/__ for instruction as to what is you will have me to do today, I wait for your orders (Proverbs 3:5-7), and I wait for your supplies (Philippians 4:19), that will enable me to carry out your will (Psalm 25:4-5). **Heavenly Father,** you are the only true source of knowledge, wisdom and goodness. I thank you for them In Jesus Name Amen. (Write down what you receive)

PLEASE NOTE while I am waiting for specifics from the Holy Spirit, I pray in the spirit so that I can hear what thus saith the Lord. There is a great danger in having our consciousness of having our Bibles, and our past experience of God's leading, doctrine, and our honest wish to do God's will, we trust in these and do realize that with every step we need and may have heavenly guidance.

B. FORGIVENESS:

(Please note that when you sin, it must be dealt with immediately, and as we continue in our daily praying, this is the point we express our sorry for any event that we did not ask for forgiveness.)

Heavenly Father, In the name of Jesus, I come before your throne of Grace "Hebrews 4:16 / Hebrews 11:6 and Matthew 6:33". I ask you for forgiveness for any sin that I may have committed, whether it be by commission or omission, I ask you to blot out any transgressions of mines (law-breaking Isaiah 43:25) and remember none of my iniquities (injustices- Hebrews 10:17). If there is anyone that may have tried to cause me any hurt, harm or danger I forgive them and release them now, I set my will to forgive at a moment's notice those who try to cause me any hurt harm or danger and sin against you.

Heavenly Father, if there is anything in my life that has not been ordered by you, or that is not entirely given up to you. I thank you for opening my eyes and showing me any areas of my life that are not pleasing to YOU. I ask you to give me strength, grace, and wisdom to change those things and remove any weight that would prevent me from having a heart to heart open relationship with You (Hebrews 12:1).

According to Psalm 139:23-24; "Search me, O God, and know my heart; Try me, and know my anxieties; and see if there is any wicked way in me and lead me in the way everlasting." Thank You for working through me to cleanse me from things that would hinder me and would give place to the devil to use as a foothold against me.

Heavenly Father, I address myself only to the true and living God and refuse any involvement of the devil in my prayer. I command you, devil, in the Name of the Lord JESUS CHRIST, to leave my presence with all your cohorts. I bring the blood of my Lord JESUS CHRIST between us. I resist all the endeavors of the devil and his cohorts to rob me of the will of God.

Heavenly Father, I come afresh this day ___/___/___ I surrender my spirit, soul "mind, will, emotions", body and my sensory mechanisms to YOU, I lay my life on the altar of consecration before YOU.

Heavenly Father, I come thanking you for your WORD, and for the leading of the Holy Spirit, desiring that your will be done in my life. I want to, be like my Lord and Savior who lived daily in the intimacy of closeness and in constant fellowship with You.

Heavenly Father, I want to know Your will more clearly, with absolute certainty of divine guidance with instructions on not only what to do, but how doing it.

Heavenly Father, work with me to do YOUR will, and to do YOUR best pleasure because for that purpose I am here in the earth only to do your will.

Heavenly Father, you are Almighty God "El-Elyon", the Most High, I bless and praise you in Jesus name, Amen.

Heavenly Father, In the name of Jesus, I take each piece of Armor, I put on YOU Lord Jesus Christ:

1. I gird my loins with the BELT OF TRUTH (Ephesians 6:14).
2. I shod my feet with the preparation of the GOSPEL OF PEACE. (2 Corinthians 5:17-21).
3. I put on the BREASTPLATE OF RIGHTEOUSNESS (1 Corinthians 1:30).
4. I put on the HELMET OF SALVATION (1 Corinthians 2:16; Ephesians 2:20).
5. I take up above all the SHIELD OF FAITH (Ephesians 6:16 / Romans 12:3, 1 John 5:4).
6. I take the SWORD OF THE SPIRIT (Hebrews 4:12).
7. I will PRAY IN THE SPIRIT (Romans 8:26-27; Jude 1:20).

Heavenly Father, I thank you that I am defensively clad with the armor of God, I am offensively equipped with the sword of the Spirit, which is the Word of God and I am empowered to successfully engage in spiritual warfare and achieve victory. Thank You for the armor of protection and surrounding me with your hedge of protection as I move forward on the spiritual battlefield (Psalm 34:7; 91:11). I am not afraid of the terror by night, the arrow that flieth by day, the pestilence that walketh in darkness; the destruction that wasteth at noonday." Thank You for allowing me to abide under the wings of the Almighty, and I say of the LORD, you are my refuge, you are my fortress, you are my source and you are my God; in you, I do trust. (Psalm 91:5-6).

I declare that the devil and all his cohorts in the spiritual realm are subject to me through the name of Jesus and by the blood of Jesus.

(Read as the Holy Spirit Leads a daily devotion on prayer: Andrew Murray, E M Bounds, and George Muller, also read from you Holy Bible 3-5 chapters per day for spiritual nourishment.)

Daily Reading: (Bible or Book) Chapters (chs) or pages (pgs.): Example Gospel of John; Mon Chs 1-3; Tue Chs 4-6; Wed Chs 7-9; Thus Chs 10-12; Fri Chs 13-15, Sat Chs 16-18, Sun Chs 19-21: (**You read Gospel of John in seven days**)

Wk1 _____, _____, _____, _____,
Wk2 _____, _____, _____, _____,
Wk3 _____, _____, _____, _____,
Wk4 _____, _____, _____, _____,
Wk5 _____, _____, _____, _____,

C. PRAYER FOR THOSE IN AUTHORITY (GOVERNMENT - FEDERAL)

Heavenly Father, I In obedience to 1 Timothy 2:1-4; your word says… "[1]I exhort therefore, that, first of all, supplications, prayers, intercessions, and giving of thanks, be made for all men; [2]For kings, and for all that are in authority; that we may lead a quiet and peaceable life in all godliness and honesty. [3]For this is good and acceptable in the sight of God our Savior; [4]Who will have all men to be saved, and to come unto the knowledge of the truth."

In 'Jesus' name I ask you for forgiveness of any sins that the nation of the United States may have committed against you. (2 Chronicles 7:14)

Heavenly Father, I ask for the healing of this nation and its land. **Heavenly Father,** I hold up in prayer before You these men and women who are in positions of authority. I believe that skillful and godly wisdom has entered into their heart, and knowledge is pleasant to them.

Heavenly Father, I ask that you compass these men and women, make their hearts and ears attentive to godly counsel, and do that which is right in Your sight.

Heavenly Father, I thank you that discretion watches over them; understanding keeps them and delivers them from the way of evil and from evil men and women. I pray that the Spirit of the Lord rests upon them, In Jesus name. (Ephesians 1:17-19)

1. (GOVERNMENT - FEDERAL)

Heavenly Father, I lift up

1. President and Family
2. Vice President and Family
3. Secretary of State and Family
4. Secretary of the Treasury and Family
5. Secretary of Defense and Family
6. Attorney General and Family
7. Secretary of Interior and Family
8. Secretary of Agriculture and Family
9. Secretary of Commerce and Family
10. Secretary of Labor and Family

11. Secretary of Health and Human Services and Family
12. Secretary of Housing and Urban Development and Family
13. Secretary of Transportation and Family
14. Secretary of Energy and Family
15. Secretary of Education and Family
16. Secretary of Veterans Affairs and Family
17. Secretary of Homeland Security and Family
18. Environmental Protection Agency and Family
19. Office of Management & Budget - Director and Family
20. US Trade Representative - Ambassador and Family
21. US Ambassador to the United Nations - Ambassador and Family
22. Council of Economic Advisers and Family
23. U.S. Supreme Court judges and Family
24. All Branches of the Armed Forces and Family
25. U.S. legislative body and Family

Heavenly Father, in the authority of the Lord Jesus Christ. I bind the devil and all his cohorts of darkness, and I render helpless principalities, powers, rulers of darkness of this world, spiritual wickedness in high places according to Ephesians 6:12 that are assigned to influence the leaders of this nation, to further the devil's agenda, In Jesus name.

(As the Holy Spirit reveals pull down the strong man for over these leaders)

2. Pray for Local Government (State)

Heavenly Father, I lift up in prayer before you the men and women who are in positions of authority in the local government. I pray and intercede for the Governors, Lieutenant Governors, State Attorney Generals, Mayors, Judges, Policemen, Fireman and their families - The State's legislative body and their families. (State House of Representatives, States senators)

Heavenly Father, I pray that each State will recognize that Israel is the chosen people of God and stand with them. I pray that the Spirit of the Lord rests upon those who are in authority in the local government. I believe that skillful and godly wisdom has entered into their heart, and knowledge is pleasant to them, Discretion watches over them; understanding keeps them and delivers them from the way of evil and from evil men and women. I believe You will cause them to be men and women of integrity.

Heavenly Father, in the authority of the Lord Jesus Christ; According to Matthew 16:19; "And I will give you the keys of the kingdom of heaven, and whatever you bind on earth will be bound in heaven, and whatever you loose on earth will be loosed in heaven."

Heavenly Father, according to Matthew 18:18; "Assuredly, I say to you, whatever you bind on earth will be bound in heaven, and whatever you loose on earth will be loosed in heaven." According to Luke 10:19; Behold, I give you the authority to trample on serpents and scorpions, and over all the power of the enemy, and nothing shall by any means hurt you.

Luke 11:20-22; But if I cast out demons with the finger of God, surely the kingdom of God has come upon you. When a strong man, fully armed, guards his own palace, his goods are in peace. However, when a stronger than he comes upon him and overcomes him, he takes from him all his armor in which he trusted and divides his spoils. (NKJV)

Heavenly Father, I bind and I render helpless all principalities, powers, rulers of darkness of this world, spiritual wickedness in high places, and the devil and all his cohorts of darkness that is assigned to the (state) of _____, cities, towns and surrounding counties. I bind and pull down the strong man and cast out of the families and each individual member of these families the spirits of poverty, lack, want, greed, selfishness, automatic failure mechanism, poor memory, confusion, anxiety and any other spirits that plague families.

Heavenly Father, in the authority of the Lord Jesus Christ, I loose in the name of Jesus in The (state) of _____, cities, towns and surrounding counties and into each family and each individual member within these families the Spirit of Deliverance, the Spirit of Adoption, each person's angel, the angel of the Lord, and the perfect labors across their path ministering your word in boldness and the power of the Holy Spirit causing these families to be saved, and that your will be done in Jesus name, Amen.

Monday	Tuesday	Wednesday	Thursday	Friday
States 01-10	**States 11-20**	**States 21-30**	**States 31-40**	**States 41-50**
01 Alabama	11 Hawaii	21 Massachusetts	31 New Mexico	41 South Dakota
02 Alaska	12 Idaho	22 Michigan	32 New York	42 Tennessee
03 Arizona	13 Illinois	23 Minnesota	33 North Carolina	43 Texas
04 Arkansas	14 Indiana	24 Mississippi	34 North Dakota	44 Utah
05 California	15 Iowa	25 Missouri	35 Ohio	45 Vermont
06 Colorado	16 Kansas	26 Montana	36 Oklahoma	46 Virginia
07 Connecticut	17 Kentucky	27 Nebraska	37 Oregon	47 Washington
08 Delaware	18 Louisiana	28 Nevada	38 Pennsylvania	48 West Virginia
09 Florida	19 Maine	29 New Hampshire	39 Rhode Island	49 Wisconsin
10 Georgia	20 Maryland	30 New Jersey	40 South Carolina	50 Wyoming

D. NATION AND PEOPLE OF ISRAEL AND PEACE OF JERUSALEM

Heavenly Father, In Jesus name I lift up in prayer before You the men and women who are in positions of authority in the nation of Israel. I pray and intercede for the Nation of Israel:

<u>Prime Minister</u>, _____, family, and Staff
<u>President</u>, _____, First Lady_____, family, and Staff
Members <u>Parliament</u> family, and Staff

I pray that the Spirit of the Lord rests upon them. I believe that skillful and godly wisdom has entered into their hearts, and knowledge is pleasant to them, discretion watches over them; understanding keeps them and delivers them from the way of evil and from evil men and women. I believe You will cause them to be men and women of integrity.

Heavenly Father, In the name of Jesus and according to Your Word; I long and pray for the peace of Jerusalem, that its inhabitants may be born again. I pray that You, Lord, will be a refuge and a stronghold to the children of Israel. Your Word says, "Multitudes, and multitudes are in the valley of decision" and whoever calls upon Your name shall be delivered and be saved. Have mercy upon Israel and be gracious to them, 0 Lord, and consider that they fight for their survival. You, Lord, are their strength and stronghold in their day of trouble. I pray that they are righteous before You and that You will make even their enemies to be at peace with them. Your Word says You will deliver those for whom we intercede, who are not innocent, through the cleanness of their hands, In Jesus name.

E. PRAY FOR THE BODY OF CHRIST AND ITS LEADERSHIP.

Heavenly Father, I lift up before you, the members of the body of Christ and its leadership: Apostles, Prophets, Evangelists, Pastors, Teachers and their families.

Example of Ministries, Church, Congregations, and Christians broadcast network:

Pastor James L. Monteria and Come and Learn of Me, Int'l and church Family,

_____/_____/_____/_____/_____/
_____/_____/_____/_____/_____/
_____/_____/_____/_____/_____.

Heavenly Father, In accordance with your Word found in Colossians 1:9-13 and Ephesians 1:17-18; I pray on behalf of my brothers, sisters and fellow members of the body of Christ, that we receive the spirit of wisdom and revelation in the knowledge of him. I thank you for our being filled with the knowledge of your will in all wisdom and spiritual understanding. The eyes of our understanding being enlightened; that ye may know what is the hope of his calling, and what the riches of the glory of his inheritance in the saints, And what is the exceeding greatness of his power to us-ward who believe, according to the working of his mighty power.

Heavenly Father, I pray that we walk worthy of the Lord and is pleasing unto you, being fruitful in every good work, and increasing in the knowledge of You Heavenly Father.

Father God, I also pray that we be strengthened with your glorious power, and that we will have all the endurance and patience as need and be filled with joy. **Heavenly Father,** I thank for our being able to share in the inheritance that belongs to your people, who live in line with your WORD.

F. PRAYER FOR OTHERS AS THE HOLY SPIRIT LEADS

Heavenly Father, In the name of Jesus I pray and thank you for the salvation:

_____,_____,_____,_____,_____,
_____,_____,_____,_____,_____,
_____,_____,_____,_____,_____
_____,_____,_____,_____,_____,

G. PRAYER FOR YOUR FAMILY

Heavenly Father, I claim your divine protection through the Blood of Jesus Christ for my spirit, my soul (mind, will, and emotions,) my body, my family, my home, my church, and my finances. In the name of Jesus, take a stand against all the workings of the devil, which would try to hinder us from serving you. I declare right now that you have not given us a spirit of fear, but of power, of love, and of a sound mind according to 2 Timothy 1:7.

1. Submitting yourself to Almighty God

I submit myself unto YOU; and I resist the devil and he must flee in the name of Jesus according to James 4:7. I refuse to fear, to doubt, to worry, to allow myself to become discouraged. I will not hate, envy, or show any type of bitterness or prejudice toward any of mankind, but I will love them with the love of God that has been shed abroad in my heart by the Holy Spirit. **Heavenly Father,** I thank You, You are the only one true living God, who has all power, and control over all things.

In Jesus name I destroy, and tear down all of the strongholds of the devil and smash all of his plans that has been formed against my spirit, my soul (mind, will, emotions,) my body, my family, my home, my church, and my finances. In the name of LORD JESUS, I now renounce, break and loose myself and family from all demonic subjection via my mother, father, grandparents, or any other human beings, living or dead, that have dominated us in any way, and I thank you, Lord, for setting us free.

3. **Breaking generational curse:** (Breaking free of evil, and generational curse on family line) -

In the name of JESUS, I now renounce, break and loose myself and my family from all psychic powers or bondages or bonds of physical or mental illness, upon me or my family line, as the results of parents or any other ancestors. I thank you Lord, for setting us free.

Heavenly Father, In the Name of JESUS, I now rebuke, break, loose myself and my family from and all evil curses, charms, vexes, hexes, spells, jinxes, psychic powers, bewitchment, witchcraft and sorcery, that have been put upon me or my family line from any persons or from any occult or psychic sources. I cancel all connected or related spirits and command them to leave us. I thank you Lord, for setting us free. I break and renounce evil soul ties that I have had or may have had with (lodges, adulterers, close friends, husbands, wives, engagements, cults, binding agreements between friends).

Heavenly Father, In the Name of JESUS, I renounce these evil soul ties; I break them and wash them away with the shed blood of the LORD JESUS CHRIST. I come to you about cursed objects and demon infestation in my home. I will clean out my house of cursed objects. I will anoint my house with oil and drive the evil spirits out of my house. Show me any cursed objects, demon infestation and spirits that need to be cast out of my home in Jesus Name.

Heavenly Father, I break the power of the spirit of divination, familiar spirit, spirit of jealousy, lying spirit, perverse spirit, spirit of haughtiness, spirit of heaviness, spirit of whoredoms, spirit of infirmity, deaf and dumb spirit, the spirit of bondage, the spirit of fear, seducing spirits, spirit of the anti-Christ, and the spirit of error. **In the name of Jesus.**

Heavenly Father, in the name of the Name of JESUS, Today I take responsibility for the effect of generational sin in my family. It was not my sin, but it is affecting me Scripture is clear that we are to repent for our father's sins and we do this today I repent, Lord, I am so sorry Please forgive me.

Lord I ask that You come in today suddenly, Lord I ask that I have a Malachi 3:1;

Experience today, which is the suddenness of God suddenly I will be healed suddenly I will be delivered suddenly. I will be set free suddenly there will be salvation in my family I speak that in faith. Today Even though I may not feel like it, I speak in faith that this will happen because God's promises are true and can affect a thousand generations... I receive my healing I receive my deliverance in Jesus' name today amen.

Heavenly Father, In the authority of the Lord Jesus Christ, I declare that my house is the Lord house. It is Bethel; it is a place of blessing. The peace of God rules and reigns here. I speak the blood of Jesus over my house. Unclean spirits shall be able to have a place in my house I cast out every spirit of strife, division, and discord. I cast out the spirit of mammon, poverty and pride.

3. Applying the Blood of Jesus over your home for Divine protection and Sleep

Heavenly Father, In the name of Jesus, I speak the blood of Jesus over my house, I speak the blood of Jesus over the North side, South side, East side, and the West side of my home, I speak the blood of Jesus over every window, every door, I speak the blood of Jesus over my entire house. In the name of Jesus, I come against every unclean spirit that would think about coming into my house and I bind them right now in Jesus name. I thank you that you give your beloved sweet sleep and I receive it right now, I rest in you Lord; I lay down in peace, and sleep, for You Lord make me dwell in safety.

Heavenly Father, your word says, let the redeemed of the Lord say so, whom you have redeemed from the hand of the enemy:
- I am redeemed by the Blood of the Lamb
- I speak the Blood of Jesus against every symptom of sickness
- I speak the Blood of Jesus over my body, I am healed
- I speak the Blood of Jesus over my doorpost
- I resist all evil with the Blood of the Lamb
- I draw a Bloodline around my work area and the devil cannot cross
- I draw a Bloodline of protection around my property and possessions I speak the Blood of the Lord Jesus Christ against any problem that I may face today
- I speak the Blood of Jesus over my home to protect all occupants and possessions from all evil
- I speak the Blood of Jesus against you devil and I declare on God's Word that it overcomes you, and you must flee.

4. Releasing the Blessing of God on yourself and Family

Heavenly Father, I invoke the blessing of the Lord that makes rich and add no sorrow. I release the presence of the Lord upon my life, my family: (spouse, children, and other family members, my grandchildren), and they shall be taught of the Lord, and great peace shall be upon them. No weapon that is formed against us shall prosper; and every tongue that shall rise against us in judgment thou shalt condemn. This is the heritage of the servants of the LORD, and their righteousness is of me, saith the LORD. In the authority of the Lord Jesus Christ I loose into *(Your Family Name) and the entire family as individuals.

The Seven Spirits of the Lord as found in Isaiah 11:2: 1. The Spirit of the Lord, 2. The Spirit of Wisdom, 3. The Spirit of Understanding, 4. The Spirit of Counsel, 5. The Spirit of Might, 6. The Spirit of Knowledge, 7. The Spirit of the Fear of the Lord

Heavenly Father, in accordance to your WORD, I also loose:
1. The Spirit of Truth,
2. The Spirit of Grace,
3. The Spirit of Life,
4. The Spirit of Sound
5. Mind, The Spirit of Inventiveness,
6. The Spirit of Love,
7. The Spirit of Joy,
8. The Spirit of Peace,
9. The Spirit of Power,
10. The Spirit of Abundance
11. The Spirit of Plenty,
12. The Spirit of Retentive Mind.

I receive in the authority of the Lord Jesus Christ into all my family members the things Jesus Christ received as the worthy lamb: power, riches, honor, wisdom, strength, blessings and the Godly inheritance of Abraham, Isaac and Jacob in the name of Jesus Christ. In the name of Jesus, I command the devil and every foul, evil spirits to lose all things that have been stolen from (Your Family Name), as well as all petroleum resources, lands, cattle, sheep, goats, oxen and anything else that the enemy has stolen. I command you devil to lose the finances of people who owe us money. I lose the angels of God to cause to come into the * (Your Family Name) treasury all moneys, lands, and other things that are ours through the blessings of Jesus Christ.

H. DAILY CONFESSION

The Law of Confession: God created this universe with words that he spoke and likewise, we are made to manifest every word that we speak. There is power in your words and you will have what you say whether it is good or bad... so watch what you say!

1. CONFESSION OF FAVOR

In the name of Jesus, I am the righteousness of God. Therefore, I am entitled to covenant kindness and covenant favor. The favor of God is among the righteous. The favor of God surrounds the righteous. Therefore, it surrounds me everywhere I go and in everything, I do. I expect the favor of God to be in full manifestation in my life. Never again will I be without the favor of God. It rests richly upon me. It profusely abounds in me.

I am a part of the generation that is experiencing God's favor immeasurably, limitlessly and surpassingly. Therefore, favor produces supernatural increase, promotion, restoration, honor, increased assets, greater victories, recognition, prominence, preferential treatment, petitions granted (prayers answered), policies and rules changed, and battles won in which I do not have to fight! The favor of God is on me and goes before me. Therefore, my life will never be the same! This is the year of God's favor in my life. That is the favor of God, In Jesus' name. Amen.

2. Confession of WHO I AM IN CHRIST

- I am blessed with all spiritual blessings in heavenly places
- I am an heir according to the promise
- I am created in the image of God
- I am delivered from the power of darkness
- I am unable to be touched by evil
- I am justified by faith
- I am blessed going in, I am blessed coming out
- I am from above and not beneath
- I am the head and not the tail
- I am an heir of God and joint heir with Jesus
- I am qualified to share in Jesus inheritance
- I am delivered from the kingdom of darkness
- I am translated into the kingdom of God
- I am transformed by the renewing of my mind
- I am strong in the Lord
- I am first and not last
- I am in God's charge; My God is working out my life with me
- I am saved by grace; I am a son of God;
- I am sanctified and set apart by the Holy Spirit
- I am chosen of God, holy and blameless before Him in love
- I am free from condemnation
- I am fearfully and wonderfully made
- I am purposely built and unique design for success
- I am forgiven of all my sins
- I am reconciled to God
- I am redeemed by the blood of Jesus
- I am a fellow citizen with the saints, the household of God
- I am a steward of great wealth
- I am chosen of God
- I am holy and blameless before Him in love
- I am established by grace
- I am an ambassador for Christ
- I am the light of the world

- I am the apple of my Father's eye
- I am filled with the Holy Spirit
- I am washed by the Word of God
- I am more than a conqueror
- I am called of God
- I am redeemed from the curse of the law
- I am spiritually circumcised
- I am God's representative in the earth realm
- I am God's workmanship, created in Christ Jesus
- I am hidden in the secret place of the Most High
- I am seated in heavenly places in Christ Jesus
- I am a partaker of His divine nature
- I am a contributing member of the body of Christ
- I am born of incorruptible seed
- I am entitled to covenant kindness and covenant favor
- I am firmly rooted, built up, and established in the faith
- I am complete in Christ
- I am healed by the stripes of Jesus Christ
- I walk in divine health
- I am protected by the angels of God
- I am a new creature in Christ
- I am the salt of the earth
- I am beloved of God; I am not my own, my body is the temple of the Holy Spirit
- I am crucified with Christ
- I am abounding in a spirit of thanksgiving
- I am the righteousness of God
- I am victorious through Christ; I am set free; I am blessed
- I am a member of a chosen generation; I am a saint; I am a visionary
- I am a part of the royal priesthood; I am fathered from above
- I am accepted in the Beloved; I am a disciple of Christ
- I am the apple of my Father's eye; I am complete in Him
- I am the bride of Christ; I am an overcomer; I am the elect of God

MONDAY - I walk in love and faith

Jesus is Lord over my spirit, my soul, and my body and I Thank You Heavenly Father that your love has been shed abroad in my heart by the Holy Spirit and that your love abides in me richly. **Heavenly Father,** I Love You, with all my heart, with all my soul, with all my strength, and with all my money-might. I Love my neighbor as myself. **Heavenly Father,** I thank you, that I am filled with YOUR fullness. I am rooted and grounded in Love. I keep myself in the Kingdom of light, in Love, in the Word, and the wicked one touches me not. I am a spirit, I have a soul, and I live in a physical body. I am in the world, but I am not of this world. I am born of the Spirit, and filled with the Spirit of God, and the Spirit of God leads me. I trust in the Lord, with all of my heart and I lean not to my own understanding. In all my ways, I acknowledge Him, and He directs my paths. My pathway is life and not death. I walk in the light of the Word of God.

The WORD of God is lamp unto my feet, Heavenly Father your WORD is a light unto my path, your WORD is food unto my spirit. Your Word shall not depart out of my mouth. I meditate therein day and night. I shall make way prosperous, and I will have good success in life. I am a doer of the Word and put your Word first. I center everything around the WORD of God. I am a believer and not a doubter. I hold fast to my confession of faith. I decide to walk by faith and practice faith. My faith comes by hearing and hearing by the Word of God. Jesus is the author and the developer of my faith. I take my shield of faith and quench every fiery dart that the wicked one brings against me. I am the just, I live by faith, and I please my Heavenly Father.

TUESDAY - I flow in the guidance of the Holy Spirit

Heavenly Father, please do not Let me miss you today, use me every day in a mighty way. Let me sense your presence and your fresh renewal every day of my life. I thank you for the memories of yesterday, but I need to experience you today, and I am expecting great things from you tomorrow. Yesterday is gone, but today and tomorrow, I live in expectation of a new and wonderful outpouring of your Mighty Spirit in my life. I am born of the Spirit, filled with the Spirit of God. The Holy Spirit dwells within me.

The Spirit of truth abideth in me, teaches me all things, and guides me into all truths. I am what the Word of God says I am, I can do what the Word of God says I can do, and I have what the Word of God says I have. I am a spirit, I have a soul, and I live in a physical body. I am in the world, but I am not of this world. I am made in God's image; I have God's nature on the inside of me. I have God's ability within me through Christ. I am working together with Christ. God's plan is for me to go forth in His ability and power.

I am bold, I am courageous, and I am a strong person. God is my Father and if He is for me, then who can be against me? Holy Spirit, You are my counselor, teaching me, educating me, training me, and develop my human spirit. Greater is He that is in me than he that is in the world. The Holy Spirit dwells within me.

WEDNESDAY - I walk in the miracle working power of God

Heavenly Father, Thank You for Your mercy and grace. I am born-again; I am filled with the Holy Spirit. I am a supernatural being, filled with the supernatural power of God; I am made in the image of God. Through the Holy Spirit within me, I have the same miracle-working power that Christ has, to do the same mighty works He did. Today, I am a believer and I am expecting His miracle power to be released within me to meet the desperate needs of those around me. Thank you that you are releasing your miracle power and other are being minister unto in spirit, soul and body by your Spirit and through your WORD.

THURSDAY - I AM healed

Heavenly Father, I bless you and I love you. I bless and love my enemies. I forgive them now and I release them in the name of Jesus. Christ has redeemed from every sickness written in the curse of the law. I am redeemed from every disease that is not written in the book of the law. Christ has redeemed me, brought me back and set me FREE from all sickness and diseases. I have been delivered from the authority of darkness. In Christ Jesus, I have redemption. I have been redeemed from captivity, I am delivered from satan dominion and his work, and I am free from sickness and disease. I am healed. I am a member of the Body of Christ. I am redeemed from the curse, because Jesus bore my sickness and carried my diseases in His own body. By His stripes, I am healed.

I forbid any sickness or disease to operate in my body. Every organ, every tissue of my body functions in the perfection in which God created it to function. I honor God and bring glory to Him in my body.

FRIDAY - All my material and financial needs are provided

Heavenly Father, Jesus has destroyed the curse over my life. Christ has redeemed me from the curse of the law. For poverty, He has given me wealth. I am prosperous, rich, and wealthy, I am out of debt and all my needs are met. I have plenty more to put in store. I sow bountifully; I reap bountifully, like a magnet, I am attracting your blessing, I am full of Joy, I am full of life, I am Healed, I am Debt Free. Lord, I acknowledge you this day. You have sent your angels unto me to walk with me. Angels walk in front of me to prepare my way; they walk behind me to protect me from area that I cannot see. They walk beside me for comfort and company. Angels are with me today. You have to promise to prosper my way. Where ever I go is prosperous, as I go I am prosperous, my way is prosperous.

Everything I put my hands to prosper, the work that I do will prosper, my career will blossom and produce fruit, and the world must make way for me; because (Your Name) in the Lord Jesus Christ, as an ambassador of the Kingdom of God is coming through. Abundance is flowing in my life from the north, south, east and west. I will not live in poverty; I will never worry about where my next meal is going to come from, or the next meal for my family. My kitchen cabinets are full, my refrigerators and freezers are full. I have all the resources that are necessary to live a life filled with abundance.

SATURDAY - I walk in the Favor and Wisdom of God

Heavenly Father, I thank you because you are doing exceedingly abundantly above all that I can ask or Think. Your mighty power is taking over in me." I am an heir of God through Jesus Christ; I am a joint-heir with Jesus Christ. I let the word of God dwell in me richly; He who began a good work in me will continue until the day of Christ. I have perfect knowledge of every situation and every circumstance that I come up against. Jesus has been made unto me wisdom, righteousness, sanctification, and redemption, I have the wisdom of God, I am the righteousness of God in Christ Jesus, and I am sanctified and sealed by the Holy Spirit. I am the redeemed of the Lord. I have an abundance of Favor flowing from God to me now, God honors me today.

I am a success today. I have God's special favor upon me today. He makes His face to shine upon me today. He is gracious to me today. I am someone very special to my **Heavenly Father,** and nothing is impossible with Him today; His favor is upon me today. I think like it, I live like it, I drive like it, and I dress like it. I am expecting great things to happen in my life today.

I obtained favor in the sight of all who look upon me. I will meet nice people today. I shall have good relationships with people today. I shall favor and honor others today. I am a blessing to the Lord. I am a blessing to others. Lord Jesus, You are my Lord and my Savior.

SUNDAY - I Walk in the Blessing

Heavenly Father, I Thank You that I am blessed because I am born into BLESSING! Thank you that the blessing is working in me, on me, and around me. I declare that I am blessed when I come in and I am blessed when I go out. Jesus came to the earth to restore the blessing that Adam lost in the Garden of Eden when he sinned. I am a child of God. I have a covenant right to the blessing. I declare that like Abraham, I am blessed to be a blessing until all the families of the earth are blessed, the blessing of God is on my life. I am empowered to prosper in every endeavor that I take on and every project that I begin. I am blessed on my job. I am blessed in all my relationships. Like Joseph, those in authority over me see the blessing of God on my life. I have favor as a result. Thanks for blessing me with all spiritual blessings in heavenly places, I am powerful, wealthy, influential and blessed! In Jesus Name, Amen

I. RETURN TO GIVING THANKS FOR THE MANIFESTATION OF WHAT

I BELIEVE THAT I RECEIVE:

Heavenly Father, I continue my offering of thanks to You. I give you praise! I am thankful and delighted to say so. I bless and praise Your name! For You are good and Your mercy and loving-kindness are everlasting. Your faithfulness and truth endure to all generations. It is a good delightful thing to give thanks to You O Most High.

Heavenly Father, again, I thank You for Your Words in Mark 9:23; Jesus said to him, "If you can believe, all things are possible to him who believes." In addition, Mark 10:27b Jesus said, "for with God all things are possible." I thank You and praise You for Your word, In Jesus name, Amen.

Heavenly Father, I worship and adore You, (El-Elyon), the Most High God, Who is the owner of everything, the Possessor of the heavens and earth. You are the everlasting God (EL-Olam), the great God, the living God, the merciful God, the faithful God, the almighty God. You are truth, justice, righteousness, and perfection. You are the Most High God (E-Elyon) the Possessor of the heavens and the earth.

Heavenly Father, I adore You, make known to You my adoration, and love for You this day. It is You Who made me, and You crowned me with glory and honor. You are the One Who is the same yesterday, today, and forever (Jehovah Shammah). You are the One Who nourishes me and provides my every need for you are (JEHOVAH-JIREH). You are my Shepherd (EL-ROHI), and I shall not want for any good or beneficial thing. You are the One Who will never leave me nor forsake me (Jehovah-Shammah).

Blessed Holy Spirit, You are my Comforter (Parakletos - one called alongside to help), You are my Spiritual Guide, and You are my Teacher.

J. Daily Confession of Protection Psalm 91 "personalize"

1. My family and I dwelleth in the secret place of the Most High; we abide under the shadow of the Almighty.
2. My family and I say of the LORD, You are our refuge and our fortress: our God; in YOU we do trust.
3. We are delivered from the snare of the fowler, and from the noisome pestilence.
4. We are covered with YOUR feathers, and under YOUR wings we trust: YOUR truth is our shield and buckler.
5. We are not afraid of the terror by night; nor for the arrow that flieth by day; Nor of the pestilence that walketh in darkness; nor of the destruction that wasteth at noonday.
6. A thousand fall by our side, and ten thousand at our right hand; but it will not come near us.
7. Only with our eyes, will we behold and see the reward of the wicked.
8. Because we have made You LORD, who is our refuge, even the Most-High, our habitation;
9. No evil will befall us, neither will any plague come near our dwelling.
10. For you have given Your angels charge over us, to keep us in all thy ways.
11. Your Angels bear us up in their hands, lest we dash our foot against a stone.
12. We tread upon the lion and adder: the young lion and the dragon we trample under feet.
13. Because we have set our love upon YOU, YOU will deliver us: YOU will set us on high, because we know YOUR **names**.

A. EL-Elyon the "Most- High God" (Genesis 14:17-20; Psalm 91:2-4, Jeremiah 32:38-40, and Psalms 21:7)
B. EL-Gmulot the "The Lord Who Rewards" Jer. 51:56, Romans 12:17-19 2 Thess. 1:6, Hebrews 10:30)
C. EL-Olam the "Everlasting God" (Isaiah 40:28-31)
D. EL-Roi "God of sight who keeps watch" (Genesis 16:13)
E. EL-Shaddai the "God, that's more than enough", the All sufficient one" (Genesis 17:1 and Psalm 91:1)
F. ELOHIM the "God that creates" (Genesis 1:1, Psalms 19:1)
G. ADONAI the "Master and owner of everything" (Psalms 24:1, Malachi 1:6)

YOU ARE JEHOVAH THE LORD, GOD, WHICH REVEALETH:

JEHOVAH "Unchangeable, "Intimate God" (Isaiah 45:21, Psalm 139:1-5)
JEHOVAH-YAHWEH "The God's of divine salvation" (Genesis 3:15, Romans 10:9-10),
JEHOVAH-TSIDKENU "The Lord our righteousness" (Jeremiah 23:5-6, 1 Corinthians 1:30),
JEHOVAH-MAkkADDESH "The Lord our Sanctifier" (Ex.31:13, Psalm 90:17, 1 Cor. 1:30, 2 Peter 1:4)
JEHOVAH-SHALOM "The Lord Our Peace and Wholeness (Judges 6:24, John 14:27)
JEHOVAH-SHAMMAH "The Lord who is Present" (Ezekiel 48:35; Psalm 16:9, 11, Hebrews 13:5,8),
JEHOVAH-RAPHA "The Lord our healer" (Exodus 15:26, Isaiah 53:5, 1 Peter 2:24),
JEHOVAH-JIREH "The Lord our provider" (Genesis 22:13-14, Philippians 4:19),
JEHOVAH-NISSI "The Lord our banner, we reign in victory" (Exodus 17:15, 1 Corinthians 15:57),
JEHOVAH-SABAOTH "The Lord of Hosts" (Isaiah 6:1-3, Romans 9:29, James 5:4),
JEHOVAH-ROHI "The Lord our shepherd" (Psalm 23:1-6, John 10:14-16, Hebrews 13:20-21);

15. We call upon You, and You will answer us: You will be with us in time of trouble; You will deliver us, and honor us.

16. With long life You will satisfy us, and show us Your salvation."

In addition, Read Luke 10:19, Matthew 18:18.

Decision Page:

Invitation: To received salvation, Fullness of the Holy Spirit, and Healing.

God's Word has the power to literally transform your life, recreate the heart of a person, change how they and secure their eternity.

To receive Jesus Christ as your own personal Lord and Savior

Are you born again? Have you ever received Jesus as your Lord and Savior? If the answer to this question is no, read these scriptures and pray this prayer, agreeing with it and believing it from your heart

John 3:16 *"For God so loved the world, that he gave his only begotten Son, that whosoever believes in him should not perish, but have everlasting life"*

Romans 10:9-10, 13 *"That if thou shalt confess with thy mouth the Lord Jesus, and shalt believe in thine heart that God hath raised him from the dead, thou shalt be saved. For whosoever shall call upon the name of the Lord shall be saved.*

For with the heart man believeth unto righteousness; and with the mouth, **Confession** is made unto salvation.

John 14:6 *" Jesus said unto him, I am the way, the truth and the life: no man cometh unto the Father, but by me.*

Pray this prayer now: Salvation

Dear God, I want to become a citizen of your Kingdom. I come to you in the name of Jesus, your son. I confess I am a sinner. I believe you sent your son to die on the cross for my sins. I confess with my mouth that Jesus Christ is Lord. Thank you for allowing me to become a Christian; I am translated from the kingdom of darkness to the Kingdom of God. In Jesus' name I pray, Amen!

A genuine born-again Christian, a citizen of the Kingdom of God wants, above everything else, to do the will of God. Do not be ashamed to witness to others and tell them how to become a Christian. Join a Bible believing Church and be water baptized as an act of faith to let the world know you are following Christ's example.

Signed_____
Date _____

If you would like to receive the Holy Spirit, ask the Father in Jesus' name to fill you with the Holy Spirit. Believe you receive when you ask and begin to speak your new language in faith as God gives it to you."

Pray this prayer now: Receive the fullness of the Holy Spirit

Heavenly Father, I come to you in faith, believing that Jesus Christ died in my place, for my sins, and arose from the dead. I ask you to fill me to overflowing with the Holy Spirit. You said in your Word that if I asked I would receive, so I ask you now to fill me to overflowing with your precious Holy Spirit. I receive Him now by faith and expect to speak with other tongues as he gives me the utterance. In Jesus' Name, Amen

Pray this prayer now: Receive healing

Heavenly Father, I pray for your healing. Put your hand on your body where you are sick and repeat this prayer: Lord Jesus you are the Great Physician. All healing comes from you. By your stripes, we are healed. I speak your Word over this body and thank you that you heal all our diseases. Thank you for healing and enabling me to walk in health. In Jesus' Name, Amen

Endnotes

1. Holy Bible (1997). Containing the Old and Test Testament Authorized King James Version Red-Letter Edition. Illinois: Tyndale House Publications.

2. Prevailing Prayer to Peace by Kenneth E. Hagin

3. A Place Called Heaven by Dr. Gary L. Wood

4. Dr. Roger Mills, *While Out of My Body I Saw God Hell and the Living Dead* (St. Clair Shores, MI: Triunity Publishing Inc., 2007)

5. Placebo by Howard Pittman, (New Philadelphian Publishing House, Foxworth, Mississippi, 1999)

About the Author

Pastor James L. Monteria is born again. Pastor Monteria to execute the call on his life attended Rhema Bible Training Center of Broken Arrow a suburb of Tulsa, Oklahoma where he earned a Diploma in Ministerial Training. He is an ordained Minister of the Faith Christian Fellowship, International of Tulsa, Oklahoma.

Pastor Monteria received his Bachelors of Science Degree in Business Administration from Saint Paul's College in Lawrenceville, VA. He received a Master's Degree in Instructional Education from Central Michigan University, Mount Pleasant, Michigan. Pastor Monteria is adjunct Professor in the community college.

Pastor Monteria has ministered the Word of God through seminars, church services, Bible studies, Prison Ministries, distribution of his books CDs and DVD. Pastor Monteria believes that the Bible is the Word of God, and he is an anointed Pastor and Teacher of the Word of God. His ministries are combinations of anointed Preaching and Teaching the Word of God and flowing in the gifts of the Holy Spirit as the lead.

Pastor J. L. Monteria is available to:
~Speaking Engagements~
~Book Signings~
~Workshops\Conferences~
Website: www.clmpublication.info
Email: clmpublication.info@gmail.com
Postal Mailing: P.O. Box 932
Chesterfield, VA 23832

www.ingramcontent.com/pod-product-compliance
Lightning Source LLC
Chambersburg PA
CBHW061308110426
42742CB00012BA/2107